So Much More than a Sing-A-Long

by Neta A. Wenrick, MS, RMT-BC

Copyright © 1996 So Much More Than A Sing-A-Long

All rights reserved. No part of this publication may be reproduced or transmitted in any form or by any means, mechanical, photographic or electronic, without prior permission in writing from the publisher.

Library of Congress Cataloging in Publication Data

Main Entry under title:

So Much More Than A Sing-A-Long

1. Music therapy 2. Activities 3. Aged 4. Nursing homes

LCCN 94-70728
ISBN 0943873-38-X

Printed in the United States of America

DEDICATION

This book is lovingly dedicated to my grandparents

Gerald Crawford

Oneta Crawford

Bruce Sluss

Joan Sluss

TABLE OF CONTENTS

Preface	iv
Autumn	1
Animals	3
Bird Call Activity	5
Inventions and Discoveries	7
Easter	10
Halloween	13
Irish Session Plan	16
Academy Awards	19
Names	21
Travel Session Plan	24
Music Session Plan	27
Disney Session Plan	34
May Day	37
A Patriotic Session	39
Childhood Memories	43
Rainbows And Clouds	45
Smiles	47
Great Songwriters	48
The Great Singers	53
More Great Musicians	57
Body Parts	59
Colonial Music	61
Cinco De Mayo	63
Country Western Music	66
Fathers And Home	68
Hawaii	70
Humor And Parody	73
Burl Ives	75
Jewish Music	76
Love Songs	78
Mardi Gras	80

Mother	82
Oriental Music	84
Trains And Railroads	86
Rain	88
The Sound Of Music	90
A Session on Spirituals	92
Springtime	94
A Session On Time	96
A Session On Weather	99
A Session On Winter	101
A Session On Summer	103
Women	105
Songs America Sang At War	108
A Session About Working	110
The 1960's	112
Using Props	114
Appendix A: Melodrama	115
Appendix B: Calendar of Sessions	121

Preface

This book provides the professional with dozens of original activities for both large and small groups. These activities have been tried and tested, and most are easily modified to fit the specific needs of any group. There are also ideas for planning sessions around specific themes. Activities and session plans follow specific holidays and events during the year.

For those who work in clinical settings, goals are provided for each activity. These are cross-referenced so that activities for a specific goal may be easily found.

I hope that this book will provide those working in the activity therapies with new ideas for planning sessions.

Activities and Sessions

Session on Autumn

Autumn is a wonderful time of the year, full of marvelous sights, sounds and smells. This is also a great time to sing songs about the Moon, since people think of Harvest Moon. A sample session follows:

1. Open the session with some recorded classical music such as Autumn from *The Four Seasons* by Vivaldi.
2. Play *Autumn Leaves* by Roger Williams, asking the group to identify the song, and possibly the artist. Ask what season is upon us.
3. Ask what happens in the Fall and sing songs accordingly. (For example, kids go back to school—*School Days*) Ask what kind of fruit is harvested. (Apples–*Don't Sit Under The Apple Tree, Ida, Sweet as Apple Cider, In The Shade of the Old Apple Tree*).

Objective:
To stimulate cognitive functioning.

4. Sing songs about the Moon.
   The following is a partial list:

   Moon River
   Shine on Harvest Moon
   Moonlight Bay
   Moonlight and Roses
   By The Light of the Silvery Moon
   My Sweetheart's the Man in the Moon
   Moon Over Miami

So Much More than a Sing-A-Long

5. Ask some "trivia questions" about the moon:
   a. What was Glenn Miller's theme song?
      (*Moonlight Serenade*)
   b. Who was the first man to set foot on the moon? (Neil Armstrong) What date? (July 20, 1969). What were his words? ("That's one small step for man, one giant leap for mankind.")

Objective:
To stimulate cognitive functioning and encourage reminiscing.

AUTUMN ACTIVITY

The following activity invites the sharing of Fall memories.

Equipment:
The only equipment needed for this activity is a portable instrument, such as a guitar.

Procedure:

1. The song below is sung once by the therapist, to the group.
2. It is then sung to each individual. Each person is asked what sight, sound or smell of autumn he or she recalls.
   If the group is large, ask participants to give some ideas.
3. This is continued until each person has had the opportunity to participate.

Objectives:
1. To provide an opportunity for reminiscing.
2. To increase verbalization.
3. To increase attention span.

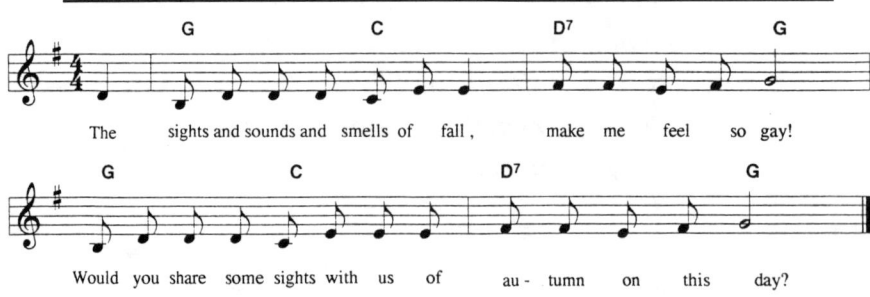

The sights and sounds and smells of fall, make me feel so gay!
Would you share some sights with us of au-tumn on this day?

Activities and Sessions

Session on Animals

A great time to do a session on animals is on February 2nd, Ground Hog Day.

1. Suitable songs for this session include:

    How Much Is That Doggie in the Window?
    O Where, O Where Has My Little Dog Gone?
    The Old Grey Mare
    Home On The Range
    Old MacDonald (They will really try to stump the leader on this one!!)
    Puff, The Magic Dragon (Although this is a children's song, everyone seems to love it.)
    Three Blind Mice (Try it in a round)
    When the Red, Red Robin Comes Bob, Bob Bobbin' Along
    Mockingbird Hill
    Mairzy Doats
    Three Little Fishies

2. Ask if anyone ever owned a pet. Try to find the most unusual pet. Snakes and monkeys were some examples my group came up with.

Objectives:
To increase verbalization and explore common interests.

3. Many phrases used in the English language mention animals. Test the group's memory by having them finish the following statements:

    a. As wise as an (owl).
    b. As clever as a (fox).
    c. As slow as a (snail, turtle).
    d. As strong as an (ox, horse).
    e. As stubborn as a (mule).
    f. As hungry as a (bear).
    g. As quick as a (fox, bunny).
    h. As thirsty as a (camel).
    i. As busy as a (bee).
    j. As happy as a (clam).

Objectives:
1. To stimulate cognitive functioning.
2. To increase attention span and encourage gross motor movement.

---

4. Rhythm activities may be done to "Alley Cat" or "BINGO" (playing the instrument when a letter is left out).

I LIKE ANIMALS

This particular activity gives a chance for the use of imagination and elicits some interesting responses:

Equipment:
No special equipment is necessary, unless the leader wants to use a tambourine for rhythm.

Procedure:
1. The leader explains that he or she is going to chant and that everyone is to participate by clapping along. Establish the rhythm first. Once everyone knows the chant they are to join in with the leader.
2. The chant at top of page 5 is done once by the leader and then again, asking one, two or more clients what animals they would like to be and why. The chant is repeated until each person has had a chance to answer.

Activities and Sessions

I like animals,
Don't you see!
If you could be an animal,
What would you be?

3. If the person is reluctant to answer, the leader might ask the group what animal that person might be. This should be done with caution and in the spirit of fun so that no one is attacked verbally or has their feelings hurt.

Objectives:
1. To provide an atmosphere for creative self-expression.
2. To encourage self-disclosure.
3. To elevate mood.

BIRD CALL ACTIVITY

There are a great many songs about birds. This topic makes a great theme for a whole session, or as part of a session on animals. The following activity is very successful and a lot of fun.

Equipment:
1. A tape recorder.
2. A tape of various bird calls. Suggested bird calls:

Canadian Goose	Barn Owl
Turkey	Blue Jay
Chicken	Crow
Seagull	Mockingbird
Mourning Dove	Robin

Whip-Poor-Will (everyone gets this one!)

Procedure:

1. The leader explains that several bird songs will be played, one at a time. The group will then have to guess which bird it is.
2. The tape is started, and each call is played one at a time.
3. After each bird call, the group is asked what kind of bird it was. If you have pictures of each bird, all the better.
4. Each individual shares something from their own experience about that type of bird.
5. This is continued as long as participants seem to enjoy it.

NOTE: There may be someone in the group who does bird calls. If so, he or she can be asked to share these with the group. See how close it is to the actual bird call.

Objectives:
1. To provide an opportunity for verbalization.
2. To increase reality orientation.
3. To provide an opportunity for creative self-expression.

Activities and Sessions

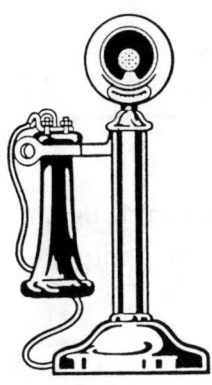

INVENTIONS AND DISCOVERIES

Columbus Day (October 12) is a difficult holiday for which to provide activities. In recent years, this holiday has been changed to "Discoverer's Day". With this in mind, the following activity focuses on various discoveries and inventions down through the years.

Equipment:

1. A portable instrument
2. A small drawstring or plastic bag.
3. Small cards with various inventions and discoveries written on them. (See page 8 for possibilities).

Procedure:

1. The leader explains that each person is going to pick a card from the bag, and read it to the group. If an individual is unable to read the card, the leader or another group member can read it.
2. That person will then tell all he or she knows about this particular invention or discovery. If the person has no information on this subject, the rest of the group can contribute what they know.
3. The person will then pick a song to go with this invention. With the help of the leader, the group sings the song. If the person cannot think of a song, the group is asked to help provide one.

So Much More than a Sing-A-Long

Objectives:
1. To provide an opportunity for choice.
2. To provide an opportunity for verbalizing.

When asked the right questions, people can come up with a surprising amount of information and reticent members get an opportunity to have input into the group.

LIST OF POSSIBLE INVENTIONS, DISCOVERIES AND SONGS

Wristwatch—Three O'Clock in the Morning

Telephone—Hello, My Baby

Cotton Gin—Pick a Bail of Cotton, Cotton Fields

Bicycle—Bicycle Built for Two

Gold in California—Oh, Susannah, California Here I Come

Hawaii—any Hawaiian song, such as Blue Hawaii

False Teeth—Smiles

Airplane—Come Josephine In My Flying Machine

Steam Boat—Cruising Down the River

Automobile—In My Merry Oldsmobile

Train—This Train Is Bound for Glory, I've Been Working on the Railroad

Eyeglasses—Ma, He's Making Eyes At Me

Baseball—Take Me Out To the Ballgame

Baby Carriage—any baby song, such as Baby Face

Gravity—Don't Sit Under The Apple Tree (Since Isaac Newton is supposed to have discovered gravity while sitting under an apple tree, this song is appropriate!)

Activities and Sessions

IF YOU COULD INVENT ANYTHING

This is a good activity to use when discussing inventions and discoveries.

Equipment:

No special equipment is needed for this activity, although the leader might want to use a drum or other rhythm instrument for support.

Procedure:

1. The leader recites the chant below to the entire group:

    *If you could invent anything at all,
    What would it be?
    If you could invent anything at all,
    What would it be?*

2. After the chant is recited by the entire group, each member is asked what one thing he or she would invent. It might be something small, like a better mousetrap, or something large, like a vaccine for peace. There will be some interesting answers!

3. This is continued until each individual has had an opportunity to participate.

4. You might use the following chant as an alternate, if the group is more frail:

    *Of all the inventions we have today,
    What is the most important you say?*

Be sure to ask why that particular invention is important.

Objectives:
1. To provide an opportunity for creative self-expression.
2. To provide an opportunity for increased verbalization.
3. To stimulate cognitive functioning.

A Session on Easter

Easter is a wonderful, reviving time of year and, although there are few Easter songs, there are many appropriate activities. One symbol of Easter is the "Easter Bonnet". The following activity makes use of this symbol.

EASTER BONNET PASS-AROUND

Equipment:

1. A portable instrument.
2. A frilly, Easter Bonnet. The "frillier" the better.

Procedure:

1. Begin by showing the group the bonnet. Sing "Easter Parade" with the entire group. Ask if anyone in the group ever attended the Easter Parade in New York.
2. Begin passing the bonnet around, while singing Easter Parade. Stop the music at intervals.
3. When the song stops, the person holding the hat must tell the group a favorite Easter story or memory. My groups have always wanted to try on the hat, even the men. If they want to do it, let them!
4. Continue until each person has had the opportunity to share.

Activities and Sessions

Objectives:
1. To encourage verbalization.
2. To give an opportunity to reminisce.
3. To encourage reality orientation.
4. To encourage gross motor movement (passing the hat around and trying it on).

MORE EASTER ACTIVITIES

1. Sing *Easter Parade* and *Peter Cottontail*. These songs have been popular with my groups.
2. Get a large stuffed rabbit (I have a terrific puppet which looks very life-like). While passing this around and giving everyone a chance to "pet" it, read *The Tale of Peter Rabbit*. It isn't long, and my experience has been that group members really enjoy hearing a familiar story. Stop and ask questions about what is coming up in the story.

Objectives:
1. To stimulate cognitive functioning,
2. To provide an opportunity for reminiscing.
3. To provide purposeful and directed sensory stimulation.
4. To encourage gross and fine motor movement.

---

3. A good song for rhythm or movement is *The Bunny Hop*.
4. Songs of inspiration are popular during Easter week. A partial list follows:

    I Believe in Music
    Sunny Side Up
    You'll Never Walk Alone
    Amazing Grace
    He's Got The Whole World in His Hands

Objectives:
To elevate mood and reduce self-pity.

Activities and Sessions

HALLOWEEN

BOBBING FOR APPLES

Halloween often holds special memories for people, especially if they were raised in a rural setting. When asked what they might have done at Halloween parties, many answer "bobbing for apples". Since the traditional way of bobbing for apples is not feasible in a health care setting, a modified version may be used.

Equipment:

1. A medium-sized basket.
2. Enough styrofoam packing "peanuts" to fill the basket 3/4 full.
3. 5-8 plastic apples (depending on the size of the group) buried in the styrofoam "peanuts".
4. A tape player and appropriate music for the session.

Procedure:

1. The music is played on the tape player.
2. The basket is taken around to each client.
3. When the music stops, the person in front of the basket is asked to reach in and find an apple. A stop watch may be used to time each person so that no one takes too long. 15 seconds is long enough for higher functioning clients while others may take up to 30 seconds.
4. The music is begun again and the procedure continues for each client. Prizes such as candy are given to those with the fastest time, and of course, everyone wins something.

NOTE: If a client does not get an apple on the first attempt, he or she is given another chance. Everyone can be successful in this activity, with a little help from the leader.

So Much More than a Sing-A-Long

Objectives:
1. To encourage gross and fine motor movement (reaching into the basket).
2. To create an atmosphere for reminiscing about childhood experiences and create group interaction.

HALLOWEEN SONG

Equipment:

The only equipment needed for this activity is a portable instrument or piano.

Procedure:

The Halloween song listed below is sung to the group. Each person is then asked to name an item they associate with Halloween. Typical answers include black cats, ghosts or trick-or-treat.

Objectives:
1. To encourage verbalization.
2. To stimulate cognitive functioning in the form of remembering and verbalizing past experiences.
3. To encourage group interaction by individual group members.
4. To elevate mood and reduce self-pity.

HALLOWEEN CAROLS AND STORIES

1. Get some "Pumpkin Carols" or Halloween lyrics set to familiar tunes. These parodies are usually popular.

Activities and Sessions

2. Read Washington Irving's, *The Legend of Sleepy Hollow*. (Get an abridged version, as it is very long). I found a very old, but very good recording of *The Legend of Sleepy Hollow* and played the last ten minutes for my groups.

Objective:
To stimulate cognitive functioning and increase attention span.

So Much More than a Sing-A-Long

Irish Session Plan

St. Patrick's Day always brings joy and fun and offers some residents a chance to share and reminisce about their Irish heritage.

1. Following is a list of well-known Irish songs for a sing-a-long:

    When Irish Eyes Are Smiling
    Sweet Rosie O'Grady
    My Wild Irish Rose
    An Irish Lullaby
    Galway Bay
    Danny Boy
    Mother MacCree
    Harrigan
    Peg O'My Heart
    Peggy O'Neil

2. A great, happy song for rhythm is *MacNamara's Band*. It also lends itself to allowing only certain instruments to play.
3. For St. Patrick's Day, we spend a lot of time listening. If you can find some John McCormack tapes, they are excellent. Bing Crosby is also a favorite.

Objectives:
1. To encourage gross motor movement and improve impulse control.
2. To provide an opportunity for reminiscing.
3. To increase cognitive functioning.

Activities and Sessions

4. Hold an Irish trivia session. Ask group members to **Name Some Famous Irish Americans**. Following is a list of some of the better known personalities.

   Andrew Jackson, president
   Ronald Reagan, president
   Woodrow Wilson, president
   John F. Kennedy, president
   Richard Daly, mayor
   Senator Joseph McCarthy
   William F. Buckley, Jr.
   John Ford, film director
   James Cagney, actor
   Pat O'Brien, actor
   Maureen O'Hara, actress
   George M. Cohan, composer
   Victor Herbert, composer

5. There is a very whimsical, and enjoyable "melodrama" about St. Patrick's day in Appendix A. Give it a try, just for fun!

TOP O' THE MORNIN'

The following activity is very enjoyable and promotes interaction among group members.

Equipment:

1. A tape player and recording of any kind of Irish music. The Irish Hornpipe works well.
2. Various rhythm instruments.

Procedure:

1. Seat group members in a circle, very close together.
2. Pass out rhythm instruments to every other person.
3. Begin the music and have the group play along with the instruments.
4. When the music stops, each person must turn to the person on his or her right and say "Top O'The Mornin". That person then gets the instrument.

5. The music is started again and the procedure continues. At some point the instruments should be passed to the left.

Objectives:
1. To increase gross motor movement by using rhythm instruments.
2. To encourage verbalization.
3. To encourage group interaction.

SOMETHIN' GREEN

When one thinks of St. Patrick's Day, the color green usually comes to mind. The following activity invites group members to name something green.

Equipment:
The only equipment needed for this activity is a portable instrument or piano.

Procedure:
1. Sing the following song to the tune of *The Wearin' of the Green:*

> *Oh, St. Patrick's Day's a big event*
> *That we all have seen.*
> *But it will be no blarney,*
> *If you'll name me somethin' green.*

2. Ask each person to name something green. Shamrocks, spinach and grass are popular answers. People often come up with very creative answers.

Objectives:
1. To stimulate cognitive functioning.
2. To encourage verbalization.
3. To create an avenue for creative self-expression.

Activities and Sessions

ACADEMY AWARDS SESSION PLAN

So many familiar songs come from movies and what better time to sing some favorites than when the Academy Awards are given out.

1. Play songs which have been nominated for an Oscar, or songs from movies which have been nominated. You will find this information in any of the books written about the Academy Awards. Here is a short list of songs:

   > *As Time Goes By* from **Casablanca** (1942)
   > *An Irish Lullaby* from **Going My Way** (1944),
   > *Que Sera Sera* from **The Man Who Knew Too Much** (1956)
   > *Moon River* from **Breakfast at Tiffany's** (1961)

2. Play *Colonel Bogey March* from *Bridge Over the River Kwai*. This is a great song for movement, particularly marching in place.

Objective:
1. To increase cognitive functioning.
2. To increase gross motor movement.
---

3. Play a game of movie trivia. There are many books where this information can be obtained. I've found that group members enjoy talking about the movies and enjoy sharing their favorites. They often have special memories.

Objective:
To increase cognitive functioning and provide an opportunity for reminiscing.
---

4. Sing the following song to the tune of *You Oughta Be In Pictures*. Then ask each person which movie star he or she would like to be, and why. Continue until each person has had a chance to answer.

*You oughta be in pictures
for everyone to see.
If you could be in pictures
Who would you be?*

Objectives:
1. To provide an opportunity for creative self-expression.
2. To increase verbalization.

Activities and Sessions

Jane Anna
Sam Shirley FRED

NAMES

A name is very special since it is carried with each person throughout life. A session devoted to names can be very rewarding and fun for all concerned.

Equipment:

1. A portable instrument.
2. A book of names, containing the origin and meaning of each.

Procedure:

1. Any of the songs on page 23 may be sung once to everyone and then to each individual.
2. As each person's name is acknowledged, read aloud from the book about its meaning and origin. If the group is very large, write out the meaning of each name before the session so that time is not wasted finding the names. In a small group, people can find their own names in the book.

Objectives:

1. To increase self-esteem by highlighting the person's name.
2. To provide an opportunity for creative self-expression by allowing people to tell the stories behind their names.

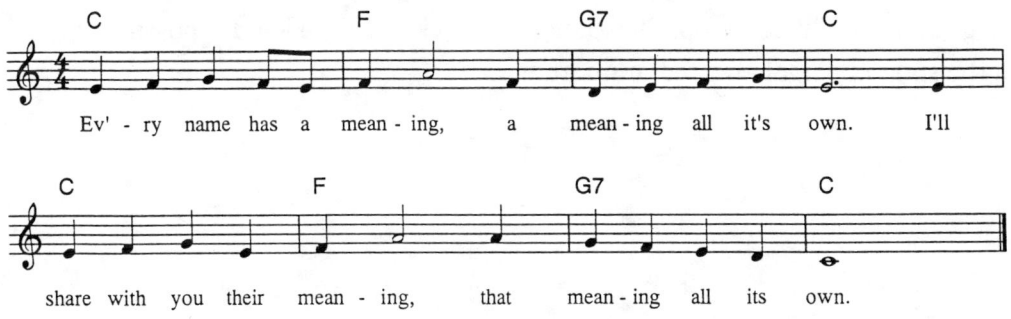

Ev'-ry name has a mean-ing, a mean-ing all it's own. I'll share with you their mean-ing, that mean-ing all its own.

"THE NAME OF OUR PLACE" ACTIVITY

Most people are proud of their homes. Even if someone is in an institution or facility, they can have pride in their surroundings. This activity is designed to use the name of the facility, thereby creating a sense of pride in it.

Equipment:

1. A blackboard, or large pad and marker.
2. A portable instrument.

Procedure:

1. Write the name of the facility vertically, down the left side of the blackboard or paper.
2. Ask members of the group to supply words describing their facility which begin with the letters on the left side of the paper. Write these beside the letter.
3. Ask group members for the title of a familiar song, such as *You Are My Sunshine* or *Springtime in the Rockies*.
4. Using this melody as a guide, take the words suggested and put them together to create a song about the facility. Write the lyrics on the board or paper. Make sure the group participates as much as possible in this process. Sometimes it is slow, but it can be very rewarding.
5. When the song is completed, sing it through several times with the entire group.
6. Make copies for the next time the group meets. Give a copy to the administrator and the activity director. This might even become the group's "theme song" to open each session.

NOTE: The spirit of this song should be positive, even though some less-than-positive suggestions might come up. These should be acknowledged and if possible, included in the song in a light-hearted, humorous way.

Activities and Sessions

Objectives:
1. To increase self esteem.
2. To increase contentment with the environment.
3. To provide an opportunity for increased verbalization.
4. To provide an opportunity for creative self-expression.

NAME SONGS

1. There is an abundance of "name" songs. You can adapt the names in these songs to those of group members. This is a good way to acknowledge each person's presence. Here is a partial list:

    If You Knew Susie
    My Little Margie
    Oh, Johnny! Oh, Johnny!
    Billy Boy
    Daisy Belle
    Mary's A Grand Old Name
    K-K-K-Katy
    My Darling Clementine
    Ida, Sweet As Apple Cider
    Wait Till The Sun Shines, Nellie
    Oh, Susannah
    Sweet Genevieve
    Cecilia

2. A great song for movement or rhythm is *Joshua Fit The Battle of Jericho*. This is a great hand-clapper. When it gets to the part which goes "And The walls came tumbling down", raise all hands in the air and bring them down in time to the music.

Objective:
To increase gross motor movement.

So Much More than a Sing-A-Long

TRAVEL SESSION PLAN

Travel is a good topic of conversation and there are many songs about travel which can be incorporated into a session. A great time to do a session on travel is in the early summer when people are beginning to take vacations.

1. Start the session by asking people about various ways they might travel and then finding a song to match. Here are some songs our group came up with:

   bicycle—*Daisy Belle (Bicycle Built for Two)*
   sailboat—*Moonlight Bay*
   train—*I've Been Working on the Railroad*
   horse and buggy—*Put On Your Old Grey Bonnet*
   horse—*The Old Grey Mare*
   taxi—*Darktown Strutter's Ball*
   car—*In My Merry Oldsmobile*

2. A good song for rhythmic activity is *Tijuana Taxi*. The Tijuana Brass version is the best.

Objective:
1. To provide an opportunity for choice and to stimulate cognitive functioning.
2. To increase gross motor movement.

Activities and Sessions

3. We also talked about places people might travel to and came up with the following:

California, Here I Come
Carolina in the Morning
Red River Valley
Give My Regards to Broadway
Sentimental Journey
Sidewalks of New York

Objectives:
1. To provide an opportunity for choice.
2. To stimulate cognitive functioning.

IF YOU COULD TRAVEL ANYWHERE

Most people have traveled at least a little in their lifetime. This activity gives people a chance to talk about their travels.

Equipment:

The only equipment needed for this activity is a portable instrument or piano.

Procedure:

1. The song below is sung once to each individual and the person is asked where he or she would like to travel, if it were possible.

25

Objectives:
1. To stimulate cognitive functioning.
2. To encourage verbalization.
3. To create an atmosphere to express unfulfilled desires.
4. To create an atmosphere for reminiscing.

EAST SIDE, WEST SIDE

This is another activity which encourages people to share their travel experiences.

Equipment:

The only equipment needed for this activity is a portable instrument, or piano.

Procedure:

1. The song below is sung to the entire group to the tune of *East Side, West Side:*

   East Side, West Side
   Everything you've seen.
   What's the best place that you have been to,
   The best place that you've been?

2. This is then sung to each individual.
3. Each person is asked to name a place to which they have traveled. They are free to share as much as they like about the trip.
4. Continue until each person has had the opportunity to participate.

Objectives:
1. To provide an opportunity for creative self-expression.
2. To provide an opportunity for reminiscing.
3. To increase verbalization.
4. To explore common interests.

Activities and Sessions

Music Session Plan

A session devoted to the theme of music can be very enjoyable. Following are some activity ideas.

1. Play songs which focus specifically on music. Here is a partial list:

   > Music, Music, Music (Put Another Nickel In)
   > I Believe in Music (great for rhythm activity)
   > Alexander's Ragtime Band (also great for rhythm activity)
   > Play a Simple Melody (this is a two part song which is really cute)
   > Singing In The Rain
   > Ja Da
   > Love's Old Sweet Song

2. *I've Got Rhythm* is a great rhythm song which can be used for individual expression or group playing.

Objectives:
To increase gross motor movement.
---

3. Get a recording of various orchestral instruments. Play a sample of each and ask the group to identify it. Then show a picture of each instrument. (I have a large chart which shows all the instruments in relation to each other so a good comparison can be made). Then ask people to name someone famous for playing that particular instrument. You'll be surprised at how much they know. So will they!!

Objectives:
To increase attention span and
to stimulate cognitive functioning.
---

4. Play "Match the Music". Give the group an artist's name and invite people to tell you the type of music for which that person is best known. For better results, play a recording of each. A partial list follows:

   Woody Guthrie, Burl Ives—folk music
   Enrico Caruso—opera
   Billie Holiday—blues
   Scott Joplin - ragtime
   Eddy Arnold, Johnny Cash - country western
   Tony Bennett - pop
   Mahalia Jackson - gospel
   Handel, Mozart - classical

Objective:
To stimulate cognitive functioning.
---

5. Conducting is a popular activity. In our group, we taught members a basic 2/2 pattern, and then conducted *Stars and Stripes Forever*. Group members enjoyed the movement. We even switched arms so that each arm got a good workout. Let group members try "conducting" with a baton as it gives more authenticity to the activity.

Objective:
To increase gross motor movement.
---

6. Some great songs for self-disclosure are *Sing* and *I'd Like to Teach the World to Sing*. These songs bring up many ideas about self-esteem and world peace and are a nice way to close a session.

Activities and Sessions

Objectives:
1. To elevate mood.
2. To reduce self-pity.
3. To provide an opportunity for self-disclosure.

JOPLIN CHANT

The Joplin Chant can be used when talking about the Gay Nineties and Ragtime music, or it can be used during a session devoted to the theme of music. Whatever the situation, I usually preface the activity with a recording of a famous Joplin piano rag, such as *Maple Leaf Rag* or *The Entertainer*. This activity gives group members more information about each other and helps them get to know each other better.

Equipment:

No special equipment is needed for this activity but you may choose to use a drum or other rhythm instrument for support.

Procedure:

1. The chant below is recited for the entire group:

   Joplin, Joplin,
   My! He could play!
   If you could choose an instrument
   What would you play?

2. The chant is then repeated to each individual.
3. Each person is asked what instrument he/she would like to play, or has played in the past.
4. Continue until each individual has had the opportunity to participate.

Objectives:
1. To increase verbalization.
2. To provide an opportunity for creative self-expression.
3. To increase self-esteem.
4. To provide an opportunity for self-disclosure.

THE DRUM IS A CIRCLE

There is something fascinating about a drum. Most everyone seems to enjoy the opportunity to play one. This activity provides that opportunity, while also fostering creative self-expression.

Equipment:

The only equipment needed for this activity is a hand drum and mallet.

Procedure:

1. The chant below is recited to the entire group:

    The drum is a circle,
    It has no end.
    Play us your rhythm
    And pass it to a friend.

2. The drum is handed to the first person in the group. The chant is then recited, with everyone participating, perhaps by clapping along.
3. The person is then asked to play his or her own rhythm on the drum. Be encouraging, no matter what is played! This is a time for exploration and self-expression, so there is no right or wrong.
4. When finished, each person is asked to whom they would like to pass the drum. It can be the person on either side, or someone across the room. If they are unable to give the drum to someone else, the leader can help.
5. The chant is repeated and the next person is asked to play a rhythm. This is continued until each person has had a chance to play the drum.

NOTE: Depending on the level of functioning, some individuals may need more assistance with this activity than others.

Objectives:

1. To provide an opportunity for creative self-expression.
2. To increase gross motor movement (playing and passing the drum).

Activities and Sessions

GRAB BAG SING-A-LONG

A sing-a-long is enjoyable and provides reality orientation as well as many other benefits. Sometimes, however, it is difficult for individuals in the group to think of songs they would like to sing "off the top of their heads". This activity gives some "hints" for songs which are common favorites, while still allowing for choice-making by individuals.

Equipment:
1. A portable instrument or piano.
2. A small bag full of cards with various words related to popular songs printed on them.

Procedure:
1. Explain that this is a sing-a-long, but that each person will be given the opportunity to choose a card from the bag. Each card has a word on it.
2. Give each person a chance to choose a card and have them read what is printed on it. Help those who need assistance.
3. The individual or group then decides on a song to fit the word drawn from the bag.
4. This is continued until each person has had at least one turn, or until the leader decides to end the activity.

NOTE: Once a card is chosen, it should be taken out of the bag and set aside, so it won't be drawn again.

Objectives:
1. To give the opportunity for choice.
2. To provide the opportunity for increased verbalization (reading the card).
3. To increase cognitive functioning.

EXAMPLES OF WORDS AND CORRESPONDING SONGS

bicycle - *Bicycle Built for Two*
yellow - *The Yellow Rose of Texas*
ain't - *Ain't She Sweet?*
game - *Take Me Out To The Ballgame*
tulip - *When You Wore a Tulip*
clover - *I'm Looking Over a Four Leaf Clover*

STOP & GO ACTIVITY

Rhythm instruments are fun to use. The following activity will add something new to a simple session.

Equipment

1. Use a variety of instruments—maracas, tambourines, claves, hand castanets—one for each person in the group.
2. Stop and go signs (2). Make two round "Stop" and "Go" signs about eight inches in diameter. Put red construction paper on one side and green on the other side of both signs. These can be put on tongue depressors or something similar.

Procedure:

1. Let each person in the group choose an instrument. Start the activity with a simple play-a-long song, to get everyone "warmed-up".
2. Show the signs to the group. Ask them what red and green signs mean when driving.
3. Let group members know that when the green sign is being shown, they must play their instruments. When the red sign is showing, they must stop.
4. Show the green sign and place the other sign behind your back. Bring out the other sign with either side showing. Continue doing this, alternating red and green signs.
5. Continue as long as the activity is being enjoyed.

Activities and Sessions

NOTE: In our group, we made a game out of this activity. I tried to catch people playing when they shouldn't have been. Group members seemed to enjoy this. The higher functioning, active clients seemed to enjoy it most.

Objectives:
1. To increase attention span.
2. To provide an opportunity for gross motor movement.
3. To provide an opportunity for "teamwork".
4. To improve impulse control.

So Much More than a Sing-A-Long

DISNEY SESSION PLAN

Nearly everyone enjoys Walt Disney movies, and songs from those movies are popular. A session on Disney works well in early December since Disney's birthday is on December 5th.

1. Begin the session with a recording of various songs from Disney films. Ask the group what these songs have in common. Once the theme is established, sing some of the songs with the group. Here are a few examples:

    Whistle While You Work
    Some Day My Prince Will Come
    Who's Afraid of the Big Bad Wolf
    When You Wish Upon A Star
    Zip A Dee Doo Dah
    Lavender Blue
    A Dream Is A Wish Your Heart Makes
    The Ballad of Davey Crockett
    Let's Go Fly A Kite
    A Spoonful of Sugar
    The Mickey Mouse Club March (M-I-C-K-E-Y)
    It's A Small World

2. A good song for a rhythm activity is *Supercalifragilisticexpealidocious* from *Mary Poppins*. It is fun and silly and people really seem to enjoy it.

Objective:
To increase gross motor movement.

Activities and Sessions

3. Movement can be done to some of the wonderful songs from *Fantasia* such as *The Waltz of the Flowers* from the *Nutcracker Suite*.

Objective:
To increase gross motor movement.
---

4. *It's A Small World* is a good closing song as it leaves everyone feeling good.

Objective:
To elevate mood and reduce self-pity.

HEIGH HO, HEIGH HO

The following Heigh Ho, Heigh Ho activity offers a good source of self-expression for group members. There are many Walt Disney songs to choose from such as *The Legend of Davey Crockett*.

Equipment:

1. A tape player.
2. A recording of *Heigh Ho, Heigh Ho*.
3. A chart with pictures of the Seven Dwarves, listing their names and characteristics. See the list at end of this section.

Procedure:

1. Show the chart to the entire group. Begin the recording.
2. Explain that each person should look at the chart and name or point to the dwarf which best characterizes him/herself.
3. Take the chart around to each individual, letting them pick out the dwarf with which they most associate.
4. Once they have picked a dwarf, ask why they picked that dwarf. You might also ask the group if they think that is most like that particular person. If not, which one would they have picked?
5. Continue until each person has had the opportunity to choose. Do not force anyone to make a choice!

Objectives:
1. To provide an opportunity for creative self-expression.
2. To provide an opportunity for self-disclosure.
3. To increase verbalization.
4. To encourage group interaction.

CHARACTERISTICS OF THE SEVEN DWARVES

HAPPY - *Pleasant*
BASHFUL - *Shy*
DOPEY - *Loyal*
SLEEPY - *Relaxed*
GRUMPY - *Skeptical*
SNEEZY - *"Nosey"*
DOC - *Leader*

May Day Activity

May Day offers a perfect occasion for a session focusing on flowers. Following are some activity ideas.

Equipment:
1. A portable instrument or piano
2. A large bag with several silk flowers:
   a. a red rose
   b. a yellow rose
   c. a yellow tulip
   d. a daisy
   e. a daffodil

Procedure:
1. Take the bag around and have someone choose a flower from it. Ask group members to identify the flower.
2. The group then chooses a song to go with that particular flower. Examples include:
   a. red rose – *Moonlight and Roses*, *Red Roses for a Blue Lady*, *My Wild Irish Rose*
   b. yellow rose – *The Yellow Rose of Texas*
   c. yellow tulip – *When You Wore a Tulip*, *Tiptoe Through the Tulips*
   d. daisy – *Daisy Belle*
   e. daffodil – *April Showers*
3. Continue the process until each person has had a chance to share.

Objectives:
1. To increase verbalization.
2. To encourage self-disclosure.
3. To reminisce about special occasions from the past.

FLOWER CHANT

This chant works well as part of a session on May Day:

> *Everyone has a favorite flower,*
> *One that they like best.*
> *Do you have a favorite flower,*
> *That you like better then the rest?*

Ask each client why that particular flower is his or her favorite.

Objectives:
1. To increase verbalization.
2. To provide an opportunity to reminisce.
3. To stimulate cognitive functioning.

MAYPOLE ACTIVITY

Maypole activities are popular. Get a large cardboard tube from a carpet store. Hang bright colored ribbons from the top. Stand it up in a bucket of sand or some other substance that will hold it fairly straight. Seat the group in a circle, giving each person a ribbon. With the assistance of the leader and others, intertwine the ribbons around the pole. Be sure to have some sprightly music playing in the background. If the group is ambulatory, have them "dance" around the pole, intertwining the ribbon.

Objectives:
To increase gross and fine motor movement.

Activities and Sessions

A Patriotic Session

Patriotic music is popular and seems to bring out the very best in everyone. The Fourth of July is the best time to do a patriotic session, although Flag Day, Memorial Day and Armed Forces Day are also appropriate times. Here are some suggestions to make this more fun and exciting.

1. Sousa marches conjure up visions of a home-town parade and flag-waving people. To create a wonderful atmosphere for sharing and reminiscing, begin a patriotic session with this music.

Objective:
To elevate mood.

2. There are so many favorite patriotic songs—everybody has at least one! Here are some popular ones:

   America
   America, The Beautiful
   God Bless America
   Columbia, The Gem of The Ocean
   Battle Hymn of the Republic
   The Star Spangled Banner
   Yankee Doodle Dandy
   You're a Grand Old Flag
   Over There

3. If this session is done on Armed Forces Day, play the Armed Forces songs. They are as follows:

   Marines -The Marine's Hymn
   Army - The Caisson Song ("what is a caisson?)
   Navy - Anchors Aweigh
   Air Force - The Wild Blue Yonder

Give people a chance to talk about their relatives in the services. This offers a great chance for reminiscing and sharing difficult information, especially if loved ones were lost in various wars. Listen sensitively as people share their memories.

Objectives:
To provide an opportunity for self-disclosure.

4. Hold a quiz on the Presidents. Work in teams to make it more of a challenge. The following are some sample questions to use:
   a. Who was the youngest President ever elected to office? (John F. Kennedy)
   b. Who was the third President? (Thomas Jefferson)
   c. Four Presidents have been assassinated. Name them. (James A. Garfield, William McKinley, Abraham Lincoln, and John F. Kennedy)
   d. Name two presidents who were former Generals. (Dwight Eisenhower and Ulysses Grant)
   e. Which president served the most terms? (Franklin D. Roosevelt)

Objectives:
To stimulate cognitive functioning.

5. Choose an appropriate song to end with. *This Land Is Your Land* is a good choice since it is a popular song and expresses many feelings. It helps unify the group, no matter what their political feelings.

Activities and Sessions

PASS THE HAT

Everyone loves to sing patriotic songs and talk about what a wonderful country we live in. This activity works well on the Fourth of July and gives group members a chance to express their patriotism.

Equipment:

1. A patriotic-looking hat, preferably red, white and blue.
2. A tape player and tape of patriotic music.

Procedure:

1. Clients are all seated in a close circle.
2. The music is started and the hat is passed around.
3. When the music stops, the person holding the hat must give one word or phrase about America.
4. This is continued until each person, including the leader, has had a chance to answer.

Objectives:
1. To encourage verbalization.
2. To provide an opportunity for self- disclosure.
3. To provide a forum for expressing patriotic emotions and feelings.
4. To reduce self-pity.
5. To elevate mood.

GEORGE COHAN

One of the most patriotic American entertainers was George M. Cohan. Most of his music is patriotic and easy to sing and his life and music provide engaging material for discussion.

1. Start the session with the Overture from the Broadway musical *George M*. The best recording is the original cast recording with Joel Grey as George Cohan.

2. The following songs can be used for a sing-a-long:
    Give My Regards to Broadway
    You're a Grand Old Flag
    Over There
    Yankee Doodle Dandy
    Harrigan (Cohan was Irish)
    Forty Five Minutes From Broadway
    Mary's A Grand Old Name
    Little Nellie Kelly

3. Use flags for a movement activity. Good songs include *You're A Grand Old Flag* and *Yankee Doodle Dandy*.

Objective:
To increase gross motor movement.

Activities and Sessions

CHILDHOOD MEMORIES

Everyone can relate to songs about childhood. This is a great session to hold at the beginning of September when schools are re-opening.

1. Suitable songs either for listening or for a sing-a-long include:

> *School Days*
> *Memories*
> *When You Were Sweet Sixteen*
> *In The Shade of the Old Apple Tree*
> *Let Me Call You Sweetheart*
> *When You and I Were Young, Maggie*
> *Little Annie Rooney*
> *Down By The Old Mill Stream*

Objectives:
1. To provide an opportunity for reminiscing.
2. To stimulate cognitive functioning.
3. To provide an opportunity for self-disclosure.

2. Try using some old favorite children's games like *This Old Man* or *The Farmer in the Dell*. I have found that when approached as "memories" these songs are not offensive. Even *Old MacDonald's Farm* is really entertaining.

Objective:
To provide an opportunity for reminiscing.

SCHOOL DAYS

Everyone can relate to the feeling of beginning school again in the Fall. This activity allows people to share about their own "school days" in a very positive, enjoyable way.

Equipment:

No special equipment is needed for this activity, although the leader may want to have a bookbag as a prop. A portable instrument such as a guitar may be useful for this activity.

Procedure:

1. The session begins with a discussion of school days and reminiscing.
2. The chant below is recited to the entire group:

    *I have a bookbag shiny and new,
    But it's empty, what do I do?*

3. The chant is then repeated for each person, asking him/her what to put into the bag. Books, pencils, and lunch are the most commonly mentioned items.

Objectives:
1. To encourage verbalization.
2. To provide an opportunity to reminisce.
3. To provide an opportunity to increase self-esteem.
4. To provide an opportunity for self-disclosure.
5. To encourage group interaction.

Activities and Sessions

RAINBOWS AND CLOUDS

There is something fascinating about a rainbow, even for an adult. Rainbows are mentioned in many songs. Here is a list of some songs which might be used:

Somewhere Over The Rainbow
Sing a Rainbow
Moon River ("...rainbow's end")
Rainbow 'Round My Shoulder
Look to the Rainbow
The Rainbow Connection
I'm Always Chasing Rainbows

There are fewer songs written about clouds. *The Silver Lining* by Jerome Kern is one which works well.

Equipment:

1. A slide projector and screen.
2. A set of slides of clouds. These can be taken during the rainy months to use in the early Spring.
3. Music for the slide show is the next requirement. *Both Sides Now* and *The Long White Cloud* by Tim Weisberg are very effective in setting the mood.

Procedure:

1. Set up the slide show before the group arrives.
2. Explain that during the slide presentation, people should concentrate on the clouds, but not comment on them. When ready, dim the lights and start the slide show with the music in the background.

3. After the slide show, go back to each slide, and ask group members to pretend they are laying in the grass watching the clouds go by, like when they were children. Ask what shapes they see in each cloud as it "drifts by."
4. Take as much time as is needed.

Objectives:
1. To provide an opportunity for creative self-expression.
2. To provide an opportunity for reminiscing and sharing.

Activities and Sessions

SMILES

The first week in August just happens to be National Smile Week (it really is!) This creates an ideal theme for a session. There are many songs written about smiling:

> *When You're Smiling*
> *Smiles*
> *Just Let A Smile Be Your Umbrella*
> *Smile*
> *Smile, Darn Ya, Smile (A really good one!)*
> *Pack Up Your Troubles in Your Old Kit Bag and Smile*
> *When Irish Eyes Are Smiling*
> *When My Baby Smiles At Me*
> *Keep Smiling At Trouble*
> *Can't Smile Without You*

Since the theme is "smiles", the main objective is to get everyone to smile. This chant works well with lower-functioning groups:

> *As small as an inch, or as wide as a mile,*
> *Won't you let us see you smile?*

Try the following with higher-functioning groups:

> *As small as an inch, or as wide as a mile,*
> *What is something that makes you smile?*

(Of course they have to smile, as well!)

Objectives:
1. To increase group interaction.
2. To improve affect.
3. To increase self-esteem.
4. To elevate the mood of group members.

GREAT SONGWRITERS

IRVING BERLIN

It is fun to "celebrate" a famous person's birthday by dedicating a session to that person's life and music. Irving Berlin, whose birthday falls on May 11th, is one such person. Here are some activities to use:

1. Berlin's music is much loved. Use some of the following songs for a sing-a-long:

    God Bless America
    Play a Simple Melody
    All By Myself
    Alexander's Ragtime Band (1919)
    Always
    Remember
    Easter Parade (1933)
    White Christmas
    Blue Skies
    A Pretty Girl is Like a Melody

2. Start the session by listening to *There's No Business Like Show Business*. Ask the group to tell you who wrote it.

Objectives:
To stimulate cognitive functioning.

3. Play a recording of Irving Berlin singing *O How I Hate To Get Up In the Morning*.

Activities and Sessions

4. Play music for rhythm activities. Catchy songs which are perfect for rhythm activities include: *Puttin' on the Ritz* and *Top Hat, White Tie and Tails*.

Objectives:
To increase gross motor movement.

GEORGE GERSHWIN

The birthday of George Gershwin, the great composer, falls on September 26th. The following activities work well as part of a session devoted to Gershwin's life and music.

1. Listen to some of Gershwin's music such as *Fascinatin' Rhythm*. Then ask the group to tell you who wrote the music.

Objectives:
To stimulate cognitive functioning.

2. Suitable songs for a sing-a-long include:

> *Swanee*
> *I Got Rhythm*
> *Embraceable You*
> *Someone to Watch Over Me*
> *I've Got a Crush on You*
> *Love Is Here to Stay*

3. Spend some time listening to *Summertime* from *Porgy and Bess* and discuss the opera. Listen to excerpts from *Rhapsody in Blue*. I was fortunate to get a recording which was made from a piano roll cut by George Gershwin himself, so we were actually hearing Gershwin play. Group members were fascinated.

Objectives:
To stimulate cognitive functioning and increase attention span.

JEROME KERN

Jerome Kern wrote lovely songs and some wonderful musicals. The following songs can be used for a sing-a-long.

> *Ol'Man River (from "Showboat")*
> *A Fine Romance*
> *The Way You Look Tonight*
> *Long Ago and Far Away*
> *Pick Yourself Up*
> *Why Do I Love You?*
> *Smoke Gets In Your Eyes*
> *I Won't Dance*
> *The Last Time I Saw Paris*
> *Who?*
> *Till The Clouds Roll By*
> *Look For The Silver Lining*

1. Fred Astaire and Ginger Rogers danced to a great deal of Kern's music. Try to find a film featuring some of their dancing.
2. Jeanette McDonald and Nelson Eddy sang many of his songs. Listen to some of their recordings of his compositions. Play the songs and ask group members to identify the singer(s).

Objectives:
1. To provide an opportunity for reminiscing.
2. To stimulate cognitive functioning.

JOHNNY MERCER

Johnny Mercer was probably the most prolific lyricist in history. He wrote hundreds of songs and contributed to 91 movie scores. His music provides a great deal of material to work with.

Activities and Sessions

1. Songs for sing-a-longs include:

    Moon River
    I'm An Old Cowhand
    You Must Have Been A Beautiful Baby
    Glow Worm
    Accentuate the Positive
    Jeepers Creepers
    Lazybones
    Goody Goody
    In The Cool, Cool, Cool of the Evening
    On the Atchison, Topeka and the Santa Fe

2. Create a trivia game about Mercer's movies. Ask who starred in the following:

    Jezebel (1938)
    Harvey Girls (1946)
    Forever Amber (1947)
    Seven Brides for Seven Brothers (1954)
    Daddy Long Legs (1955)
    Peter Gunn (1959)
    Breakfast at Tiffany's (1961)
    Pink Panther (1964)
    The Great Race (1960)

Objective:
To stimulate cognitive functioning.

3. Good songs for rhythmic movement from Mercer's collection include *The Strip Polka* (Andrews Sisters version), *In The Cool, Cool, Cool of the Evening*, or *Goody, Goody*.

Objective:
To increase gross motor movement.

4. *Skylark* is a song that Mercer wrote with Hoagy Carmichael. Linda Ronstadt made a particularly lovely version which is great for singing, listening, or easy, expressive movement.

Objectives:
To increase attention span and/or
increase gross motor movement.

5. Another beautiful song which Mercer wrote along with Henry Mancini is *"The Sweetheart Tree"*, from *The Great Race*. This is also a lovely song for listening or expressive movement.

Activities and Sessions

THE GREAT SINGERS

Al Jolson, Bing Crosby and Judy Garland are some of the best remembered of the great singers.

THE MUSIC OF AL JOLSON

Al Jolson did some wonderfully singable music. Most of his music is well known and well loved.

1. Begin the session by listening to one of his lesser known songs, then ask the group to identify the singer. Since his voice is easily identified, they usually have no trouble.

Objectives:
To stimulate cognitive functioning.

2. His songs include:

> *April Showers*
> *Baby Face*
> *California, Here I Come*
> *Hello, My Baby*
> *Carolina in the Morning*
> *Ida, Sweet as Apple Cider*
> *If You Knew Susie*
> *Sitting on Top of the World*
> *Mammy*
> *Swanee*
> *Toot, Toot, Tootsie*
> *When The Red, Red Robin Comes Bob,*
>   *Bob Bobbin' Along*
> *Rock-A-Bye Your Baby With A Dixie Melody*
> *The Anniversary Song*

3. Play a song for rhythmic activity. *Waiting for The Robert E. Lee* is a happy, lively song for movement.

Objective:
To increase gross motor movement.

4. Jolson made some wonderful recordings, but probably his most famous is *Sonny Boy*. See if the group can identify this most famous song before it is played.

5. Trivia about Jolson's life is fascinating. Who was his wife? (Ruby Keeler). What was his trademark saying? ("You ain't heard nothin' yet."). What was his real name? (Asa Yoelson).

Objectives:
To stimulate cognitive functioning and provide an opportunity for reminiscing.

THE MUSIC OF BING CROSBY

Since Bing Crosby was Irish and since there is so much Irish music in his repertoire, a session revolving around his music is often popular around St. Patrick's day.

1. Play one of Crosby's songs and ask group members to identify him. Since his voice is so easily recognized, use a song that is not too familiar. Then play his theme song, *When the Blue of the Night Meets the Gold of the Day*. This beautiful song generates a good response.

Objective:
To stimulate cognitive functioning.

Activities and Sessions

2. Popular sing-a-long songs include:

   Swinging on a Star
   True Love
   Accentuate the Positive
   Pennies from Heaven (1932)
   Dear Hearts and Gentle People
   White Cliffs of Dover
   Million Dollar Baby
   It's Been a Long, Long Time
   Don't Fence Me In
   Blue Skies
   White Christmas
   An Irish Lullaby

3. Have a trivia game revolving around Crosby's life. There are several books available which are good sources for trivia questions about his life and movies. Make a game out of naming his family members, his movies, and his Oscar nomination.

Objectives:
1. To stimulate cognitive functioning.
2. To provide an opportunity for reminiscing.
3. To increase verbalizing.

THE MUSIC OF JUDY GARLAND

Although Judy Garland had a tragic life, she left some wonderful music behind. A session on her music and movies provides a great reminiscing experience.

1. Start by listening to *You Made Me Love You* and ask the group to identify the singer. This song is a little difficult to recognize, but most people get it fairly quickly.

2. Hold a trivia session about Garland's life. Together, group members may be able to name her many films (35 in all). *The Wizard of Oz* is probably her most famous. Here are some ideas for trivia questions:

a. What was Judy Garland's real name? (Frances Ethel Gumm)
b. Who was her co-star in the Andy Hardy movies? (Mickey Rooney)
c. Who were her co-stars in *The Wizard of Oz*? (Ray Bolger, Jack Haley, Bert Lahr, Margaret Hamilton, Billie Burke and Frank Moore). Can group members name each one's character in the movie?
d. What year was it made? (1939, same as *Gone With The Wind*)
e. In what movie did she play a waitress? (*The Harvey Girls*, 1946)
f. Who were her co-stars in *Easter Parade*? (Fred Astaire, Ann Miller, Peter Lawford)
g. Who wrote the music? (Irving Berlin)

Objectives:
To stimulate cognitive functioning, increase verbalizing and provide an opportunity for reminiscing.

3. Songs suitable for sing-a-longs include:

You Made Me Love You
Zing, Went the Strings of My Heart
I'm Just Wild About Harry
I'm Always Chasing Rainbows
I Got Rhythm
Smile
Rock-A-Bye Your Baby with a Dixie Melody
When You're Smiling
For Me and My Gal
When You Wore A Tulip
Meet Me In St. Louis
Under The Bamboo Tree
On The Atchison, Topeka and the Santa Fe
Easter Parade

Activities and Sessions

>*In The Good Old Summertime*
>*Get Happy*

4. Good songs for rhythm activities include: *Get Happy, Chicago,* or *Zing, Went the Strings of My Heart.*

Objectives:
To increase gross motor movement.
---

5. Judy Garland's theme song, *Over The Rainbow,* can be used to close the session.

MORE GREAT MUSICIANS

NAT KING COLE

Nat King Cole made many recordings and there are several books on his life where you can find enough information to create a complete session. The following songs can be used for a session.

>*Honeysuckle Rose*
>*I Can't Give You Anything But Love*
>*Embraceable You*
>*Paper Moon*
>*I'm In The Mood For Love*
>*When I Take My Sugar To Tea*
>*Yes Sir, That's My Baby*
>*Walkin' My Baby Back Home*
>*Down By The Old Mill Stream*
>*Smile*
>*Ramblin' Rose*
>*Those Lazy, Hazy, Crazy Days of Summer*

THE MILLS BROTHERS

Following is a list of songs which can be used to develop a session about the Mills Brothers.

> *Glow Worm*
> *Satin Doll*
> *Paper Doll*
> *Up A Lazy River*
> *Moonlight Bay*
> *You Tell Me Your Dream*
> *Daddy's Little Girl*
> *You Always Hurt The One You Love*
> *Sweet Leilani*
> *Linda*
> *Any Time*
> *My Mother's Eyes*

THE ANDREWS SISTERS

The Andrews Sisters recorded some wonderful songs which may be easily adapted for a sing-a-long.

> *Don't Sit Under The Apple Tree*
> *Apple Blossom Time*
> *Boogie Woogie Bugle Boy*
>   (A great song for rhythm activities)
> *Beer Barrel Polka*
> *Strip Polka* (also great for rhythm)
> *Oh, Johnny, Oh, Johnny*
> *Rum and Coca-Cola*
> *Bei Mir Bist Du Schon*

Activities and Sessions

BODY PARTS

The theme of "body parts" makes an interesting subject for a session. Here are some ideas:

1. Start the session by mentioning various body parts and finding songs to match. Here are the songs our group came up with:

    Heart
    After The Ball
    Moonlight Bay
    Peg o' My Heart
    Heart of my heart

    Head
    Show Me The Way To Go Home

    Brain
    Casey (The Band Played On)

    Face
    Singin' In The Rain
    Put on A Happy Face
    Baby Face

    Arms
    Oh, You Beautiful Doll

    Toe
    Tiptoe Through the Tulips

    Eyes
    Ma, He's Making Eyes At Me
    When Irish Eyes Are Smiling
    Green Eyes
    Beautiful Brown Eyes

2. Movement activites like *The Hokey Pokey* or *Simon Says*, which name specific body parts are excellent for use in this session.

Objectives:
To increase gross motor movement.

3. Create an Orff Chant to go with the session:

   "If you were a body part, what would it be?"
   (repeat)

This will give everyone the opportunity to express themselves in a funny, creative way. In our group, some people wanted to be eyes so that they could see everything, while others wanted to be ears. It was very interesting, and revealed a lot about group members.

Objectives:
1. To provide an opportunity for creative self-expression.
2. To provide an opportunity for self-disclosure.
3. To create an opportunity to verbalize.

Activities and Sessions

COLONIAL MUSIC

It is difficult to find enough music to cover a holiday like Thanksgiving. Since the first Thanksgiving was celebrated in Colonial America, I looked up some familiar songs which came from that period. It was interesting to find out what the Pilgrims might have been singing to the Indians on that first Thanksgiving in 1621.

1. Begin by listening to some colonial music. The lyrics are often quite funny. People relish the opportunity to hear new kinds of music as they soon tire of over-used songs like *Let Me Call You Sweetheart*.

2. Here is a list of songs which may be used for a sing-a-long:

    Shady Grove
    Simple Gifts
    Amazing Grace
    I Know Where I'm Going
    The Bluebells of Scotland
    Soldier, Soldier Won't You Marry Me
        (A really fun one!)
    Green Grow the Lilacs
    I Gave My Love a Cherry (The Riddle Song)
    Paper of Pins

3. The dulcimer was a popular instrument in Colonial America. If you, or a group member can play the instrument, all the better. It is a simple, drone instrument and group members may be able to play simple accompaniments.

Objectives:
1. To help increase self-esteem.
2. To encourage creative self-expression.

4. Mother Goose Nursery Rhymes came from this period (1719) and are fun to recite. See how many rhymes group members can recall. Some have been set to music and can be sung with the entire group. Find out if group members had favorite nursery rhymes as children.

Objective:
To provide an opportunity for reminiscing.

5. End this session with Thanksgiving songs such as *Over The River* and *Come Ye Thankful People*. The whimsical melodrama in Appendix A that deals with Thanksgiving is also worth trying.

Activities and Sessions

CINCO DE MAYO

If you don't live in California, you might not be familiar with Cinco de Mayo, (the Fifth of May). In Mexico, this is the celebration of the nationals driving the French out of the country (not to be confused with Mexican Independence Day on September 16th). This holiday gives a good opportunity for a session with Mexican/Latin American Music. I always bring in a Mexican flag, a sombrero (hat), and some other Mexican artifacts to make the session more festive.

1. To get everyone in the mood for a fiesta (celebration), begin this session with festive Mariachi music.

Objective:
To elevate mood.

2. As a "hello" song, I put the following new words to *La Cucaracha*. Teach this song to the group so they can sing along:

> *Buenos Dias mi amigos,* (Good Day my friends)
> *I'm so happy that you've come here.*
> *Buenos Dias, mi amigos,*
> *Hope you have a lot of fun here.*

Objectives:
To increase verbalization and increase group interaction.

3. The following songs are suitable for this session:
    La Cucaracha
    Tangerine
    La Bamba
    Green Eyes
    Ramona
    Maria Elena
    My Adobe Hacienda

4. Mexican rhythm instruments are easily obtained and easy to play. Maracas, claves, a guiro and hand castanets can be used for rhythm activities. Pass them around and have group members identify each one. Play along to more mariachi music and ask them to identify some of the instruments heard in this music — the guitar, a bass guitar, and trumpet are some commonly used examples.

Objectives:
1. To increase attention span.
2. To stimulate cognitive functioning.
3. To increase gross motor movement.

5. A favorite song is the *Mexican Hat Dance* or *La Raspa*. Bring a sombrero and let everyone take turns "stomping" in tune to the music. The dance can be modified for a large group by putting the sombrero in the middle and just doing hand and feet movements to the music.

Objective:
To increase gross motor movement.

6. In keeping with the festive atmosphere, bring in some Mexican sweet bread (pan dulce) for group members to taste.

Activities and Sessions

7. Ask people to name some famous Mexican Americans. Examples include: Lee Trevino, Anthony Quinn, Vicki Carr, Trini Lopez, Cesar Chavez, and Pancho Gonzalez.

Objective:
To stimulate cognitive functioning.

8. *Vaya Con Dios* is a good closing song.

Although festive music is new to many people, it is usually very well received. Plan in advance to dress everyone in festive attire. The colors for Cinco de Mayo are red, green and white—the colors of the Mexican flag. The more festive and bright the session, the better it is for the group.

Country Western Music

Country/Western music is a truly American musical genre. No where else in the world is there anything quite like it. Some facilities have a month or a week when they "go country" and it is nice to do this session during that time.

    1. A great song to open the session is *Foggy Mountain Breakdown*. This is a lively song and always gets everyone in the mood.

Use the original Flatt and Scruggs version, if you have it.

Objectives:
To elevate mood.

    2. Here is a partial list of sing-a-long songs for this session:

You Are My Sunshine
Home on the Range
Daddy Sang Bass
The Green, Green Grass of Home
Cool Water
King of The Road
Mockingbird Hill
Are You Lonesome Tonight?

3. A special tribute to Hank Williams can include the following songs:

   Jambalaya
   Your Cheatin' Heart
   Cold, Cold Heart
   Hey, Good Lookin'
   I Saw The Light

4. Play more country music and have the group identify some of the instruments such as the guitar, steel guitar, bass, mandolin, banjo, and fiddle.

Objective:
To stimulate cognitive functioning and increase verbalization.

5. While seated, have the group do some "wheelchair square dancing" to the tune of *The Old Red Wagon*. You can also use *Skip to My Lou* or any other square dance song. Find out if group members ever square danced.

Objective:
To increase gross motor movement.

6. End the session with *Happy Trails*. See if people can tell you who wrote it. (Dale Evans Rogers).

Fathers and Home

Taking time to talk about Fathers is very important. This session can bring long-forgotten memories of fathers to mind. Since it is often difficult to find songs for Father's Day, combine songs about Fathers and songs about Home.

1. Some songs worth considering for a sing-a-long include:

    Fathers
    I Want A Girl
    Daddy's Little Girl
    O My Papa
    Home
    Home on the Range
    Home Sweet Home
    Anyplace I Hang My Hat Is Home
    Dear Hearts and Gentle People (hometown)

2. Take the tune to "M-O-T-H-E-R" and have the group create lyrics to go with F-A-T-H-E-R instead. Have them match the letters to words, just as in the first song. It will be very interesting to see what they come up with. Record their suggestions, and keep a copy for the future.

Objectives:
1. To stimulate cognitive functioning.
2. To provide an opportunity for self-dislcosure.
3. To provide an opportunity for creative self-expression.

Activities and Sessions

3. We spend a lot of time talking about mothers and sometimes fathers are neglected. Use the following chant to give each person an opportunity to talk about their father.

    Father, daddy, papa, dad.
    Give us one word about your Dad

Objectives:
1. To provide an opportunity for self-disclosure.
2. To increase verbalizing.

HOME

This activity revolves around home and can be done individually or with the entire group, depending on their functioning level.

1. Place the word H-O-M-E across the top of a large sheet of paper. Down the left side of the paper, place four categories as follows:

    H   O   M   E

    A piece of furniture — hat rack
    or appliance in the HOME

    An adjective that
    describes HOME

    A type of plant — oleander
    found at HOME

    A type of food
    served at HOME

2. Have the group fill in each blank with a word beginning with the letters above. Examples are shown. You will be surprised by some of the answers.

HAWAII

Hawaii is a fascinating place which many group members may have visited. Even if people haven't been to Hawaii, it is wonderful to imagine being there. This session is usually full of beautiful memories and lovely music.

1. Begin the session with Hawaiian background music.
   101 Strings has a beautiful relaxing tape which you might try.
2. Show a map of Hawaii to the group and see what facts they can tell you about the state. The following are some interesting facts:

   50th state
   Admitted August 21, 1959
   state flower — hibiscus
   state song — Aloha Oe

Objective:
To stimulate cognitive functioning.
---

3. See if group members can name any of the eight islands:
   (Oahu, Hawaii, Maui, Kahoolawe, Lanai, Molokai, Kauai, Niihau).
4. Some songs appropriate for sing-a-long are as follows:

   Hawaiian Wedding Song
   Tiny Bubbles
   Beyond the Reef
   Sweet Leilani
   Blue Hawaii
   Harbor Lights
   Red Sails in the Sunset
   Pearly Shells
   Lovely Hula Hands
   Hawaiian War Chant
   My Little Grass Shack

Activities and Sessions

5. Use guided or "unguided imagery"— giving the group a scene and letting their imaginations guide them. Again, the *101 Strings Album* has some lovely imagery-type songs. People who have been to Hawaii can draw on their experiences. Those who haven't been know enough about the islands to let their imagination take them someplace beautiful and exotic. Discuss what was seen and felt and what smells were experienced.

Objective:
To provide an opportunity for self-disclosure and reminiscing.

6. The music of Hawaii is very unique. If a ukulele is available and if you or someone in the group can play it, so much the better. If you have any authentic Hawaiian instruments, show them to the group and demonstrate how they are used. You have to learn first! Percussive instruments such as claves and rhythm sticks are good for Hawaiian music and can be used for a rhythm activity.

Objectives:
1. To increase gross and fine motor movement.
2. To stimulate cognitive functioning.
3. To increase attention span.

7. Do the "wheelchair hula", using only the hands and upper body. Teach group members some basic hand motions and then "hula" to a familiar Hawaiian song. A really good one with easy hand motions, is *Hukilau*. It is a good form of exercise and every now and then someone really tries to hula!

8. If you can get some fresh pineapple and/or coconut, let group members try to open it! Sugar cane will also add to the atmosphere. Taste experiences (as well as musical and visual ones) really enhance a session about Hawaii.

Objective:
To provide purposeful and directed sensory stimulation.

9. Close with *Aloha Oe*.

Activities and Sessions

HUMOR AND PARODY

The second week in April is National Laugh Week. This is a great week to do a session on Humor and Parody. There are nearly as many parodies as there are legitimate songs. This week offers people a chance to laugh together and tell silly jokes and stories.

1. Begin the session by listening to a silly song by Danny Kaye or something "classical" like *Dance of the Comedians* from *The Bartered Bride*.

Objective:
To elevate mood.

2. Here is a list of songs which are good for sing-a-longs:

   On Top of Spaghetti (tune: *On Top of Old Smokey*)
   Parodies on *"Let Me Call You Sweetheart"*
   Parodies on *"Daisy Belle"*
   Parodies on *"My Bonnie"* (there are many!)
   Parodies on *"Mary Had A Little Lamb"*
   What Did Delaware? (an old camp song)

3. For a rhythm and self-disclosure activity, I created the following Orff chant:

   Play us a silly, sound, a funny sound,
   a silly sound.
   Play us a silly sound on your instrument.

Group members select an instrument of their choice while the chant is sung.

So Much More than a Sing-A-Long

Objectives:
1. To provide an opportunity for gross motor movement.
2. To promote self-disclosure and creative self-expression.
---

4. A "Comedian Quiz" will give people an opportunity to reminisce. Here are some sample questions:

   a. This was a husband and wife team. He's still around, smokes a big cigar. Her last name was the same as Jack Benny's rival. (George Burns and Gracie Allen)

   b. Which comedian played a violin, had a butler named Rochester and a wife named Mary? Phil Harris, Don Wilson and Dennis Day were on his radio show. He had a running feud with Fred Allen. (Jack Benny)

   c. What lady was popular in the Ziegfeld Follies. On radio, she was "Baby Snooks". Two movies starring Barbra Streisand were made about her life—*Funny Girl* and *Funny Lady*. (Fanny Brice)

   d. This team consisted of a gentleman and a "wooden friend". The friend now resides in the Smithsonian Institute. (Edgar Bergen and Charlie McCarthy).

   e. Which comedian was fond of golf and teamed with a certain singer for many years to make movies? He is most famous for his USO shows overseas. (Bob Hope)

   f. Name the red-headed comedian who starred in *White Christmas* and was famous for his "way with words"? (Danny Kaye)

   g. Name the team which made it big in radio, but also made many films together. One was tall and thin, the other short and fat. One of their most famous routines was "Who's On First". (Abbott and Costello).

Objective:
To stimulate cognitive functioning.

Activities and Sessions

   5. After this quiz, I usually play a tape of Abbott and Costello's routine "Who's On First". Since it isn't very long, most groups find it very enjoyable.

> **Objective:**
> To provide an opportunity for reminiscing.

BURL IVES

A session can be devoted to the wonderful folk songs popularized by Burl Ives.

   1. Begin the session by playing a Burl Ives tape and asking the group to identify the singer. His voice is easily recognized.

> **Objective:**
> To stimulate cognitive functioning.

   2. The following recorded songs are suitable for sing-a-longs:

   Red River Valley
   Oh, Susannah
   Shenandoah
   Barbra Allen
   Blow the Man Down
   Cockles and Mussels
   Big Rock Candy Mountain
   Go Tell Aunt Rhody
   The Blue Tail Fly
   Lavender Blue
   Hush Little Baby
   Tom Dooley
   Sweet Betsy from Pike

   3. Songs which can be used for rhythm activities include *You Are My Sunshine* and *My Pony Boy*.

> **Objective:**
> To increase gross motor movement.

Jewish Music

There are many Jewish holidays during the year. Rosh Hashonah, which usually falls in September, can be used to teach the group a little about the holiday and to play music from *Fiddler on the Roof*.

1. Begin by playing recorded traditional Jewish music and ask group members to identify it. Tell them a little about Jewish holidays and culture.

Objective:
To stimulate cognitive functioning.

2. There are a few Jewish folk songs which are easy to teach. One is *Zum Gali Gali*. This is easy to learn because it is repetitive.
3. A wonderful Jewish song for rhythm activities is *Hava Nagila*. This lively song gets everyone moving. Those who know the words can sing along.

Objective:
To increase gross motor movement.

4. Hold a "Who Am I?" Quiz about famous Jewish Americans. Following are some sample questions:
   a. I discovered the theory of relativity and received a Nobel prize. (Albert Einstein)
   b. I also received a Nobel prize, but for helping fight polio in this country. (Jonas Salk)
   c. I was a composer and wrote such masterpieces as *Rhapsody in Blue* and *Porgy and Bess*. (George Gershwin)

Activities and Sessions

    d. I wrote many songs, but the most well known is *God Bless America*. (Irving Berlin)

    e. I am a comedian, smoke a big cigar and my wife and partner was Gracie Allen. (George Burns)

    f. I was a comedian and forever 39 years old. I was also very thrifty. (Jack Benny)

    g. I was a very popular singer in the 1920's and 1930's. I wore a black face and liked to sing of *Mammy*. (Al Jolson)

Objective:
To stimulate cognitive functioning.

---

5. *Fiddler on the Roof* is a wonderful play. Try to get the movie cast recording or the original Broadway cast recording with Zero Mostel.

6. Songs for a sing-a-long include:

> *Sunrise, Sunset*
> *Matchmaker, Matchmaker*
> *If I were A Rich Man* (good rhythm activity)
> *Tradition* (good for listening and discussion about values and traditions)
> *Sabbath Prayer* (provides insight into some Jewish customs)

Love Songs

There have probably been more love songs written than any other type of song. Valentine's Day is always special because there is such a vast repertoire of songs to choose from. A sing-a-long list is not included in this section since there are so many love songs, most of them very well known.

1. Open the session with some romantic music and talk about the history of Valentine's Day. If you can get some old Valentine cards, it makes the discussion more interesting.

2. Use Stevie Wonder's song *I Just Called to Say I Love You* for a rhythmic activity. I've found that group members enjoy new music, especially if it is melodic and has a nice message, like this one does.

Objective:
To increase gross motor movement.

3. Below you will find **The Great Lovers' Quiz** which I developed for my groups. Ask group members to provide the name which will complete each pair.

   Antony and (Cleopatra)
   Romeo and (Juliet)
   The Duke of Windsor and (Wallis Simpson)
   Napolean and (Josephine)
   Prince Charles and (Princess Diana)

Activities and Sessions

> *Prince Andrew and (Princess Sarah)*
> *Robin Hood and (Maid Marion)*
> *Scarlet O'Hara and (Rhett Butler) – from which movie?*
> *Mary Pickford and (Douglas Fairbanks)*
> *Mary and (Joseph)*

Group members may be able to come up with other famous lovers to add to the list.

Objectives:
1. To stimulate cognitive functioning.
2. To provide an opportunity for creative self-expression.

4. If there are folks in your groups who were born in different countries, they can probably still speak a second language. Try to get a list of many different ways to say "I love you" from these different cultures. This gives people a chance to share their culture and to express feelings and thoughts they may not often get to share.

Objective:
To provide an opportunity for self-disclosure and group interaction.

5. *Let Me Call You Sweetheart* is a good song to end the session with.

Mardi Gras

Even if you cannot make it to New Orleans, you can still celebrate the festive occasion of Mardi Gras.

1. To set the mood, open the session with some Dixieland music. Party hats, streamers, balloons, and masks all help create a festive mood.

Objective:
To elevate mood.

2. Ask if anyone in the group has ever been to New Orleans, or to the Mardi Gras. Invite those who have been to relate their experiences.

Objectives:
To provide an opportunity for self-disclosure and reminiscing.

3. "Party" type songs for a sing-a-long include:

Roll Out The Barrel
Alexander's Ragtime Band
Darktown Strutters Ball

Activities and Sessions

4. Color works well for this session. Use brightly colored scarves for movement and play another Dixieland song.
5. *When the Saints Go Marching In* is a happy, lively song to end the session with and everyone joins in clapping and singing. It leaves the group on a positive note.

Objectives:
To elevate mood and reduce self-pity.

MOTHER

Mother's Day is a terrific holiday. Most people enjoy songs about mother and it is a subject to which everyone can relate.

1. Begin this session with a good recording of a "mother" song such as the Mills Brothers' version of *My Mother's Eyes*.
2. Give people a little history about Mother's Day.
3. Some well known songs include:

    I Want A Girl Just Like The Girl
    My Mammy (get Al Jolson's recording)
    That Wonderful Mother of Mine
    M-O-T-H-E-R (when singing this song, ask about other qualities in a mother)
    Mother MacCree

4. Create a chant which will give everyone an opportunity to share something about their mother:

    Mothers are special,
    Yes it's true!
    What is something special
    your mother gave to you?

The "something special" can be a value, attitude, or special heirloom.

Objectives:
To provide an opportunity for self-disclosure, reminiscing and increased verbalization.

Activities and Sessions

5. Since mothers and babies go together, I usually play some songs with "baby" in them:

> *You Must Have Been A Beautiful Baby*
> *I Found A Million Dollar Baby*
> *Baby Face*
> *Pretty Baby*
> *Yes Sir, That's My Baby*
> *My Blue Heaven*

6. Lullabies work well for creative movement. They are soft and soothing, and make a nice background for fluid, easy motions.

Objective:
To increase gross motor movement.

ORIENTAL MUSIC

Oriental music is beautiful and offers a new listening experience for many people.

1. Begin the session by listening to Japanese or Chinese music. James Galway and other artists have recorded albums of Japanese music.

2. Songs appropriate for sing-a-longs include:

    Far Away Places
    On a Slow Boat to China
    Japanese Sandman
    Poor Butterfly
    It Looks Like Rain in Cherry Blossom Lane

Although these are not really Oriental songs, they have the flavor of Oriental music and are quite easy to sing.

3. Use fans for a movement activity. There are so many lovely Japanese melodies that any number can be used for movement.

Objectives:
To increase gross and fine motor movement.

4. Since Oriental culture may be foreign to many group members, this session offers a good opportunity to expose people to oriental culture and oriental food. For a really nice touch, serve rice cakes and tea (oolong or jasmine). You can continue listening to Oriental music while enjoying these goodies.

Activities and Sessions

Objective:
To provide purposeful and directed sensory stimulation.

5. Oriental instruments are much different than Western instruments and group members find it interesting to see pictures of instruments found in the East. Contrast these to Western instruments and let the group hear examples of each, if possible. Then use very percussive instruments for rhythmic activities, to simulate some of the Oriental sounds. If you can bring in instruments such as a koto, shamisen, and shakuhachi, all the better.

Objectives:
1. To stimulate cognitive functioning.
2. To increase gross motor movement.

Trains and Railroads

A session devoted to trains guarantees a great deal of excitement. Nearly everyone has traveled on a train and some have very vivid memories of such travel.

1. There are so many wonderful songs about trains. Here are a few:

    Wabash Cannonball
    Sentimental Journey
    Atchison, Topeka and the Santa Fe
    Get On Board, Little Children
    This Train is Bound for Glory
    The Rock Island Line
    Hallelujah, I'm A Bum
    Big Rock Candy Mountain

2. A great song for rhythmic activity is *The City of New Orleans* by Willy Nelson. The rhythm of the song makes it seem as though you are really on a train.

Objective:
To increase gross motor movement.

3. Discuss railroad words such as the following:

    butcher boy
    caboose
    round house
    sidetrack
    wrong side of the tracks
    double header – a train with two engines
    gandy dancer – tramps and hobos who worked on the railroad

Activities and Sessions

4. Discuss the Harvey Girls and the role they played in railroad history and the history of this country.

Objectives:
1. To stimulate cognitive functioning.
2. To increase verbalization.
3. To provide an opportunity for reminiscing.
---

5. Guided imagery works well for this session. There are numerous recordings of train sounds available. Use these to let groups reminisce about some of their own experiences on a train. Have them share with the group, anything they "saw" or experienced in their imagination.
6. A good song to end the session with is *This Train is Bound for Glory.*

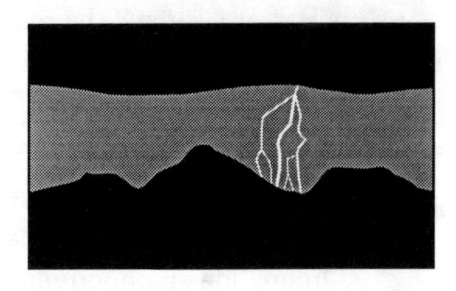

RAIN

APRIL SHOWERS

There are many wonderful songs about rain which make for mellow and relaxing listening.

1. Here are some popular songs for a sing-a-long:

    Singing in the Rain
    Just Let A Smile Be Your Umbrella
    April Showers
    It Looks Like Rain in Cherry Blossom Lane
    Pennies from Heaven

2. Use guided imagery. There are many tapes available with rain sounds such as *Meadow in a Rainstorm*. Have the group listen and then tell what they heard and saw. Since many residents no longer have a chance to see or hear the rain, this will provide a pleasant and rare experience. Avoid anything with a lot of thunder. A little bit can make the session more interesting and generate wonderful discussions.

Objective:
To provide an opportunity for self-disclosure.

3. Rain affects everyone in a different way and each person has special feelings regarding rainy weather. Here is a chant to help people express what they feel about the rain:

    The Rain comes down.
    Play us a sound,
    That tells us how you feel
    When the rain comes down.

Activities and Sessions

Each person uses an instrument to express how they feel and the group "guesses" the emotion expressed by each individual. Have a good selection of soft, loud, bright and mellow instruments available.

Objective:
To provide an opportunity for self-disclosure and group interaction.

The Sound of Music

Rodgers and Hammerstein wrote some wonderful musicals. Their most famous is probably *The Sound of Music*. Using songs from the show, I created a session which was informative and fun for my groups.

1. Begin by playing the overture to the *Sound of Music* and have the group name the musical and the composer. Group members are usually able to do this.

Objective:
To stimulate cognitive functioning.

2. Give people a little history about the story and show them a picture of the real von Trapp family. This is quite eye-opening since Maria von Trapp looks nothing like Julie Andrews and the Captain did not look like Christopher Plummer!

3. Some songs appropriate for a sing-a-long are:

   The Sound of Music
   Edelweiss
   My Favorite Things (You might ask the group to name some of their favorite things)
   Do-Re-Mi

4. I used the recorded version of *The Lonely Goatherd* (recorded version) for rhythmic activities. We only played during the yodeling.

Activities and Sessions

Objective:
To increase impulse control and attention span.

5. A great inspirational song is *Climb Every Mountain*. This is good for listening and discussion and makes a good song to close the session with.

Objectives:
To elevate mood and reduce self-pity.

A Session on Spirituals

One of our great American treasures and a truly American musical genre is that of the Spiritual. There are so many that it is hard to choose just a few. This session is suitable for use during the week of the observance of Martin Luther King, Junior's birthday.

1. Play an album of great spirituals. I used one by Tennessee Ernie Ford as an introduction to the session. Pick the lively ones to begin the session.

2. Choose hand-clapping, toe-tapping songs for a sing-a-long.

3. *When The Saints Go Marching In* is great for rhythmic activity. If you find a good recording, use it. Everyone seems to enjoy this song and I use it often in my sessions.

Objectives:
1. To stimulate cognitive functioning.
2. To increase gross motor movement.

4. *Down By The Riverside* is a great song for self-disclosure. Sing it through once and then ask group members what "burden" they would lay "down by the riverside". This activity was very successful with a stroke rehabilitation group. Many group members said they would lay down their cane or walker. It was very encouraging and gave everyone the hope that someday those burdens might really be laid aside. This is a good song to close the session with since it is uplifting and positive and leaves everyone with a note of hope.

Activities and Sessions

Objectives:
1. To reduce self-pity.
2. To provide an opportunity for self-disclosure.

SPRINGTIME

Spring is a wonderful, refreshing season and everyone looks forward to this renewing time of year. There are some terrific songs which relate to this season, even though they do not mention it specifically.

1. Begin the session with some classical music. (I try to expose my groups to classical music whenever possible). *Spring* from *The Four Seasons* by Vivaldi is a bright, happy melody. *Spring* from Tchaikovsky's *The Seasons* is also a good opener.

2. Here is a partial list for sing-a-long songs:

    Springtime in the Rockies
    April Showers
    Sunny Side Up
    California, Here I Come
    Zip A Dee Doo Dah
    I'm Looking Over a Four Leaf CLover
    Oh, What a Beautiful Morning
    While Strolling Through the Park One Day

3. Ask the group what type of sports are played in the Spring. They will invariably say baseball. This is a cue for *Take Me Out To The Ball Game*.

Objective:
To stimulate cognitive functioning.

4. Great songs for movement include *Voices of Spring* or *Tales of the Vienna Woods* by Johann Strauss. They are fairly long,

Activities and Sessions

which gives ample opportunity for movement. I often find my groups humming along with the music. Sometimes I use brightly colored scarves to represent the bright, beautiful colors of Spring.

5. For a rhythmic activity, I often use *Red, Red Robin*. The Al Jolson version is best.

Objective:
To increase gross motor movement.

6. Spring brings out some wonderful memories and feelings. I use the following chant to give individuals a chance to share their feelings with the entire group:

> *Springtime is a wonderful thing.*
> *What comes to mind when you think of Spring?*

Objectives:
To provide an opportunity for self-disclosure and increased verbalization.

7. Since Spring is the season for weddings, we often sing love songs. Here is a sample list:

> *For Me And My Gal*
> *Sitting on Top Of The World*
> *I Love You Truly* (I ask if this was sung at anyone's wedding)
> *Let Me Call You Sweetheart*
> *My Blue Heaven*

8. This might be a good session to incorporate some "Bird" songs.

A Session on Time

Time is an essential part of our lives and there are many songs which relate to Time. This session can be used when the time is being changed (e.g. Daylight Savings Time). People enjoy the novelty of focusing on this topic.

   1. To introduce the subject of time, open the session with Ragtime music and ask the group to identify it. Tell group members that you are going to focus on songs that relate to time. Talk about daylight savings time with all its benefits and difficulties.

Objectives:
To provide an opportunity for self-disclosure and increased verbalization.
---

   2. Songs for a sing-a-long can be divided into several categories as follows:

General:

After the Ball
Any Time
As Time Goes By
Always
Now Is The Hour

Morning:

Oh, What A Beautiful Morning
Good Morning

Activities and Sessions

Afternoon:
> *Cruising Down the River (On A Sunday Afternoon)*
> *On a Sunday Afternoon*

Sundown (Twilight):
> *Twilight Time*
> *At Sundown*

Evening/Night:
> *It's A Grand Night For Singing*
> *Last Night On The Back Porch*

Late Evening:
> *Sleepy Time Gal*
> *Three O'Clock In The Morning*
> *Good night, Sweetheart*

3. Suitable songs for rhythmic movement include: *One O'Clock Jump* and *The Syncopated Clock* by Leroy Anderson. These are fun because you can use very percussive instruments such as woodblocks to simulate a clock.

Objective:
To increase gross motor movement.
---

4. Most people have a favorite time of day. The following chant gives group members an opportunity to talk about their favorite time of day:

> *Morning, afternoon or night,*
> *What would you say*
> *If I asked you to tell me*
> *Your favorite time of day?*

Ask group members why that time is their favorite. This gives everyone a chance to learn something new about each other.

5. A variation on the previous activity is to provide a tray of various instruments and ask each person to pick an instrument and "play" how they feel at some particular time of the day. This is also a good self-disclosure activity for use with non-verbal group members.

Objective:
To provide an opportunity for self-disclosure.

Activities and Sessions

A Session on Weather

Although a previous session focused on "Rain", this session which incorporates all types of weather, is also very effective. Here are some suggestions.

1. Songs for a sing-a-long may be broken up into various types of weather conditions as follows:

Snow:
>   *Let It Snow!*
>   *Winter Wonderland*
>   *Sleigh Ride*
>   *Jingle Bells*

Sunshine:
>   *Wait Till The Sun Shines, Nellie*
>   *You Are My Sunshine*
>   *On The Sunny Side of the Street*
>   *Sunny Side Up*
>   *My Old Kentucky Home*

Rain:
>   *Just Let A Smile Be Your Umbrella*
>   *Singing In The Rain*
>   *Pennies From Heaven*
>   *April Showers*

Wind:
>   *Button Up Your Overcoat*
>   *Blowin' In The Wind*
>   *My Bonnie*

Clouds:
> *Look For The Silver Lining*
> *Blue Skies*
> *Home on the Range*
> *It is Well With My Soul (a beautiful old hymn)*

2. Simulate the sound of rain with rhythm instruments. Begin with maracas as the sound of rain. Add tambourines to simulate thunder and finally use the drums as a loud clap of thunder. Use your imagination and encourage group members to do the same.

Objectives:
1. To increase gross motor movement.
2. To increase attention span.
3. To provide an opportunity for creative self-expression.

3. Use the instruments for "Sleigh Ride" for another rhythmic activity. Use sleigh bells to make it more realistic and fun. Woodblocks are great to simulate horses' hooves.

Objectives:
1. To increase gross motor movement.
2. To provide an opportunity for creative self-expression.

4. I usually close this session with *Look For The Silver Lining*, as it is a positive, encouraging song with a wonderful message. We often talk about it before we finish the session.

Objectives:
1. To elevate mood.
2. To reduce self-pity.
3. To provide an opportunity for self-disclosure.

Activities and Sessions

A Session on Winter

Since the beginning of winter is so close to Christmas (December 22), carols are suitable for use in this session.

1. Begin the session with the Winter section from *The Four Seasons* by Vivaldi.

2. Suitable songs for a sing-a-long include:

    Button Up Your Overcoat
    Cuddle Up A Little Closer
    Will You Love Me In December As You Do In May?

3. If you can get a recording of a snowstorm or blizzard, use it for a short guided imagery. People who have been in a snowstorm can share their experiences with the group. This is a great activity for self-disclosure.

4. Winter is a popular season for many activities which cannot be enjoyed at any other time of year. The following chant encourages the sharing of activites which are specific to Winter:

    The snow is on the ground.
    It's Winter all around.
    Tell us what you like to do
    When the snow is on the ground!

Objectives:
To provide an opportunity for increased verbalization and self-disclosure.

5. Encourage group members to discuss what winter is like in various parts of the country. Many of them may come from various parts of the country and it is interesting to hear their perspectives on Winter.

Objective:
To provide an opportunity for reminiscing.

6. A good song for rhythmic movement is *Troika* from *The Seasons* by Tchaikovsky. It is very realistic in simulating a sleigh ride.

Objective:
To increase gross motor movement.

Activities and Sessions

A Session on Summer

Summer is a really enjoyable time of year, with everyone on vacation and many leisure activities available. A session devoted to this time of year is enjoyable and helps elicit happy memories of the early years.

1. To set a carefree atmosphere, open the session with happy, holiday-type music, such as calliope music.

Objective:
To elevate mood.

2. Play *The Summer Knows* or *A Summer Place,* and ask the group to identify the song and the session's theme.

Objective:
To stimulate cognitive functioning.

3. Here are some suggestions for sing-a-long songs:

   In the Good Old Summertime
   Think Summer
   The Lazy, Hazy, Crazy Days of Summer

4. There are some wonderful beach stories which deserve telling. Using the song *By The Sea* as a lead-in to talk about the beach, I brought out my very large beach ball (4 feet in diameter) and gave the group a chance to kick and hit it around the circle. Although everyone gets a little wild sometimes, this activity is really enjoyable and causes many memories of childhood and vacations to surface.

5. Pinwheels are a useful prop for this session. We enjoyed running them through the air and blowing on them.

Objectives:
1. To increase gross motor movement.
2. To provide an opportunity for self-disclosure and reminiscing.

Activities and Sessions

WOMEN

In August the ratification of the 19th Amendment to the Constitution, giving women the right to vote, is celebrated. Sometime during the month of August, hold a session devoted to songs written by women (either words or music or both).

1. Begin the session by discussing the 19th Amendment. In my group, many people remembered the ratification and told wonderful stories.

Objective:
To provide an opportunity for reminiscing.
---

2. Burl Ives did an album of folk songs about women. Use this to introduce the session, or just to open a discussion about how songs concerning women have changed.

3. Here is a list of songs which were written in part or in whole by women:

>*I Love You Truly* - Carrie Jacobs Bond
>*Shine On Harvest Moon* - Nora Bayes Norwortth (music)
>*Pick Yourself Up* - Dorothy Fields (words)
>*It's a Good Day* - Peggy Lee (words)
>*I'm in the Mood For Love* - Dorothy Fields (words)
>*The Sunny Side of the Street* - Dorothy Fields (words)
>*Springtime in the Rockies* - Mary Hale Woolsey (words)
>*Beautiful Ohio* - Mary Earl (music)
>*When the Moon Comes Over The Mountain* - Kate Smith

So Much More than a Sing-A-Long

Battle Hymn - Julia Ward Howe (words)
Let Me Call You Sweetheart - Beth Whitson (words)
America, the Beautiful - Katherine Lee Bates
Sweet Rosie O'Grady - Maude Nugent
Hello, My Baby - Ida Emerson (music)
I Can't Give You Anything But Love - Dorothy Fields
Three O'Clock in The Morning - Dorothy Terriss
Cruising Down the River - Eily Beadell and
  Nell Tollerton

Objective:
To stimulate cognitive functioning and increase verbalization.

4. A quiz focusing on great women can be done in teams or individually. Here is a quiz which was well received by my groups.

   a. Who was the youngest First Lady? (Jacqueline Kennedy)

   b. Who wrote Gone With The Wind? (Margaret Mitchell)

   c. Who wrote The Tales of Peter Rabbit? (Beatrix Potter)

   d. Who was dubbed "The Swedish Nightingale"? (Jenny Lind)

   e. Who was the first Black woman in Congress? (Shirley Chisholm)

   f. Who wrote Uncle Tom's Cabin? (Harriet Beecher Stowe)

   g. Who founded the Red Cross? (Clara Barton) When? (During the Civil War)

   h. Who was a temperance leader in this country? (Carrie Nation)

   i. Who discovered radium? (Madame Curie)

   j. Who created a great wax museum in London? (Madame Tussaud)

   k. Who was the first woman Prime minister of the following countries: India? (Indira Ghandi) Israel? (Golda Meir) England? (Margaret Thatcher)

   l. During the Civil War, who established the Underground Railroad to help slaves escape to the North? (Harriet Tubman)

Activities and Sessions

m. Who wrote *Little Women*? (Louisa May Alcott)

n. Who was the first women to fly solo across the Atlantic? (Amelia Earhart) What happened to her? (She disappeared).

Objectives:
To stimulate cognitive functioning and increase verbalization.

Songs America Sang At War

Although war is not a pleasant subject, it is a fact of life. Times of war produce some wonderful music. For Armed Forces Day, I created a session devoted to Songs America Sang While At War.

1. I began the session with some recorded music from the Civil War.
2. The songs for this session were broken up according to wars, as follows:

Civil War:
- Dixie
- Johnny Has Gone for A Soldier
- The Yellow Rose of Texas
- Marching Through Georgia
- The Caisson Song
- The Battle Cry of Freedom

World War I:
- Over There
- Long, Long Trail
- Smiles
- Pack Up Your Troubles In Your Old Kit Bag
- How Ya Gonna Keep 'Em Down On The Farm
- My Buddy
- K-K-K-Katy
- It's A Long Way To Tipperary
- Mademoiselle From Armentiers
- You're A Grand Old Flag
- Keep The Home Fires Burning

Activities and Sessions

World War II:

The White Cliffs of Dover
God Bless America
I'll Be Seeing You
Don't Sit Under The Apple Tree
Now Is The Hour
It's Been A Long, Long Time
Till We Meet Again

3. Play a recording of Irving Berlin singing *Oh How I Hate To Get Up In The Morning.* It will greatly add to this session.
4. *Boogie Woogie Bugle Boy* by the Andrews Sisters is a great song for rhythmic activity. Everyone usually ends up singing along.

Objective:
To increase gross motor movement.

A Session About Working

Celebrate Labor Day by holding a session devoted to work. Everyone has worked at some time in their life, even if they say they were "only a housewife". This session promotes discussion about people's lives and is a good session for self-disclosure.

1. There are many songs about work. A particular favorite is *Working On The Railroad*.

2. After singing some songs about work, I asked each person in the group what they had done for a living. After we learned about peoples work lives, we tried to find songs to match those lines of work. Here are some of the songs we sang:

    Teacher: Schooldays
    Dogcatcher: Oh Where Has My Little Dog Gone
    Housewife: This Is The Way We... (Children's game)

Let group members use their imagination to come up with whatever they find appropriate. In our group, one person had been a cement finisher. The group came up with the song *Sidewalks of New York*. It was perfect!

Objectives:
1. To provide an opportunity for choice.
2. To stimulate cognitive functioning.
3. To increase verbalization.
4. To increase group interaction.
5. To provide an opportunity for self-disclosure.

Activities and Sessions

3. *The Typewriter* by Leroy Anderson has the sounds of a manual typewriter and is a good song for movement. When I used this recording with a group, we pretended to be typing along with the music. As well as being fun, this activity provided a good movement for fingers, and hands too!

Objective:
To increase gross and fine motor movement.

THE 1960'S

Music from the 1960's tends to be overlooked in music therapy sessions. The focus tends to be on music from the Gay Nineties, the 1920's, 1930's, 1940's and 1950's. Some really great music came from the sixties and this session can be devoted to the music and events of that era.

1. Begin by playing music from the 1960's. Then ask the group to identify the era.

Objective:
To stimulate cognitive functioning.

2. Here is a partial list of songs for a sing-a-long.

Moon River
King Of The Road
Sunrise, Sunset
People
Red Roses For A Blue Lady
New World In The Morning
Dream A Little, Dream of Me
I Left My Heart In San Francisco
Try To Remember
What The World Needs Now
Blowin' In The Wind
The 59th Street Bridge Song (Feelin' Groovy)
He Ain't Heavy, He's My Brother
Bridge Over Troubled Water

Activities and Sessions

3. *Those Were The Days* is a good song for rhythmic movement as it starts slowly and picks up speed.

Objectives:
To increase gross motor movement.

4. Talk about the events of the 1960's. Most people have some interesting experiences and insights to share. Many of my group members were raising children or grandchildren during the 1960's, so the music is familiar to them. Talking about this time can provide an opportunity for healing and self-disclosure.

Objectives:
To provide an opportunity for verbalization and self-disclosure.

5. *Puff, The Magic Dragon* is a good song to finish the session with. It is nostalgic and fun for everyone.

Using Props

Music and movement go naturally together. I have found that by using props along with the music, individuals move much more freely and easily. Below you will find suggested uses for these props.

Christmas Activity

For movement I used a very shiny, soft, many-colored tree garland. With clients seated in a circle, I gave each person part of the string of garland, making sure there was plenty of "slack" between each person. Then using recorded Christmas music, we did various movements while holding onto the garland. It worked very well and seemed to be well received by the group.

Cinco De Mayo

Using brightly colored scarves and "bullfight" music, we used the scarves as capes and moved as though we were participating in a bullfight. We even shouted "Toro" and "Olé" once in a while.

Oriental

Small fans can be used for gentle and graceful movements to oriental music.

Summertime

Early in the Summer, large, brightly colored pinwheels can be used. We used these for movement with music and also blew on them to get people to breathe deeply. It was really fun. No one wanted to give them up at the end of the activity.

For Fourth of July, we used flags on a two-foot stick. These were just the right size. We waved them to patriotic music, such as *Stars and Stripes Forever*. This was very well received.

Activities and Sessions

APPENDIX A

MELODRAMAS

This appendix describes two whimsical melodramas which work well with low- and high-functioning groups. The group leader is the Narrator and reads the skit. All individuals participate; some are assigned the main parts, while others are "extras". Props such as hats, crowns and bowls are used and each character is given a rhythm instrument. Instead of having the characters "speak" their parts, each one plays their instrument.

The leader reads the melodrama. When the leader comes to the speaking part for each character, he or she mentions that person's name and reads the dialogue. Whenever their character is mentioned, that person plays the instrument. The technique of having each person "play" their part, rather than speak it, works very well, especially for people who have poor eyesight and cannot read well, or those who have little speech. Try to give each person an instrument which "matches" the character they are portraying (for example, give a drum to the Indian Chief).

How The Turkey Became The Official Thanksgiving Bird

This is a fractured bit of history about the first Thanksgiving feast, and how the first turkey ended up on the table.

The cast of characters (and I do mean characters!!) is varied:

John Pilgrim, our pilgrim father
Priscilla Pilgrim, our pilgrim mother
Anna Pilgrim, our pilgrim daughter
Charlie Pilgrim, our pilgrim son
Chief Sitting Pretty, our Indian chief
The Indian Brave, Running Slow
Various Pilgrims and Indians attending the feast

The fractured tale opens in the kitchen of the cozy Pilgrim house, the day before the first Thanksgiving feast. Priscilla and Annie are in the kitchen busily preparing for the next day's festivities. John and Charlie are "busy" in the living room, discussing the next day's activities:

> John: Well, son, tomorrow we will be making history by celebrating the very first Thanksgiving.
>
> Charlie: Why will we be making history?
>
> John: Why, without Thanksgiving, there will be no major holidays between Fourth of July and Christmas!

(Priscilla enters)

> Priscilla: John, have you killed the pig for tomorrow's feast?
>
> John: (suddenly meek) Not yet, dear.
>
> Priscilla: Well— go get it done! Now!!
>
> John: (again meek) Yes, dear.
>
> Charlie: Can I help, Father?
>
> John: Okay, let's go get it over with.

Priscilla turns to Annie who has just entered the room:

> Priscilla: Your father is so lazy! I have to make sure he does everything.
>
> Annie: Yes, Mother.

Just then, the door flies open and John comes running in with Charlie behind him:

> John: Something terrible has happened! Our pig has been...stolen...he's gone!
>
> Charlie: Just vanished!
>
> Priscilla: Gone! Now what are we going to do? There goes our meal. It's ruined.
>
> Annie: And Chief Sitting Pretty is going to be mad because we don't have ham and pork chops. Boy, are we in trouble!
>
> Charlie: We'll all be scalped!

Just then we hear a knock at the door (knock, knock, knock):

> John: I'll get it. Maybe someone is returning our pig.

He answers the door and his expression turns to one of great fear. It's Chief Sitting Pretty.

> Chief: How!
>
> Charlie: How, what?
>
> Chief: How are the preparations coming for the feast tomorrow? My braves and I are looking forward to that delicious ham and those wonderful pork chops.

Appendix A

Annie: Oh no!

John: Well, Chief, we have a small problem. Our pig has been...uh...misplaced.

Chief: Misplaced? Well, I hope you find him by tomorrow. I am counting on it.

Priscilla: Well, Chief, we'll do our best.

Chief: You'd better! (He leaves)

Priscilla: What are we going to do, John? We have to have something for tomorrow's feast.

John: Can't you make a pot of stew or something? Maybe that will appease them?

Priscilla: I'll try it.

Charlie: Boy, are we in trouble!

The scene closes.

The second scene opens the following day, at the feast. Everything looks and smells wonderful, even the squirrel stew that Priscilla has prepared to appease the Indians. There are various Pilgrims standing around making noises.

John: I sure hope this works.

Annie and Charlie: Me too!

Priscilla: We'll just have to wait and see.

Just then, the Chief enters with all of his Indian braves following behind:

Chief: John: Did you find that pig?
John: Well, not exactly, Chief, but Priscilla has made something very special for the feast—squirrel stew. I guess we will just have to take care of this!

All the Indians begin making war-like noises. John, Priscilla, Annie, Charlie and the rest of the Pilgrims are frightened (make frightened noises). Suddenly a noise comes through the forest. It is Running Slow, the Indian Brave. He's dragging something behind him.

Running Slow: What is all the noise about?

Chief: What are you dragging behind you?

> **Running Slow:** Some stupid bird! I was out hunting squirrels and this dumb bird got in the way of one of my arrows. (Running Slow is not a very accurate shot anyway!). What a turkey!
>
> **All:** Turkey!
>
> **John:** That's it! We'll have turkey for Thanksgiving!
>
> **Chief:** A Wonderful idea.
>
> **Priscilla:** That's a stupid idea! How can we go down in history as having had turkey on the first Thanksgiving? People will laugh at us for generations!
>
> **Charlie & Annie:** They'll laugh at us for years and years!
>
> **John:** They will just have to get used to the idea.

Everyone shouts and cheers because Running Slow has saved the day and the first Thanksgiving. Thus ends our fractured tale...and now you know why we serve turkey instead of pork chops on Thanksgiving.

How St. Patrick Drove The Snakes from Ireland

This is a fanciful melodrama about how St. Pat drove the snakes from the Emerald Isle.

Cast of characters:

St. Pat *Leprechaun King*
Leprechauns *Mrs. St. Pat*
Snake Queen *Snakes*
Palace guard

Our story begins many years ago on the Emerald Isle. St. Pat had become well-known for being very kind and good-hearted. As we begin, we find St. Pat at home in his easy chair in front of the fireplace, reading the evening paper. Mrs. St. Pat is in the kitchen peeling potatoes. We hear a knock at the door (knock, knock).

> **St. Pat:** Would you get that, honey. I'm busy.
>
> **Mrs. St. Pat:** Yes, dear! (she comes running from the kitchen with a potato in her hand). As she opens the door, we hear her say: Oh, good evening, your Highness. Do come in.

The Leprechaun King enters.

Appendix A

Leprechaun King: Good evening, Mrs. St. Pat. Thank you for inviting me in. I will leave the other leprechauns outside.

We hear protests from the other leprechauns. I need to see St. Pat.

St. Pat has left his paper and is coming to greet the King.

St. Pat: Good evening, King Leprechaun. What can I do for you?

Leprechaun King: St. Pat, you really must do something about all these snakes! They are terrorizing the leprechauns, especially the ladies and children. They must go!

St. Pat: But what can I do?

Leprechaun King: You are such a wise and powerful man that surely you can think of something. If you don't, you will have a leprechaun revolt on your hands!

Mrs. St. Pat: Oh, dear! Not That! Pat, do something!

St. Pat: Well, I'll give it a try. Give me a week.

Leprechaun King: You have one week. I must be going.

He heads for the door, opens it and announces to the leprechauns: St. Pat is going to drive the snakes away within the week.

The leprechauns cheer. He leaves.

St. Pat: How in the world am I going to get rid of all these snakes? What have I gotten myself into?

Mrs. St. Pat: You'd better think of something quickly. You only have a week.

SCENE 2

The next morning, St. Pat heads for the Snake village. As he enters, he is confronted with a large group of snakes. They start hissing at him to leave, but he says:

St. Pat: Please take me to your Queen. I must speak with her immediately.

Reluctantly, they noisily take him to the Queen's palace. The guard stops St. Pat.

Guard: What do you want?

St. Pat: I must see the Queen. I have important business. I represent the King of the Leprechauns.

Guard: In that case, follow me. As he approaches the Queen, he says: Announcing St. Pat, representing the King of the Leprechauns.

Queen: Come closer, St. Pat. How can I help you?

St. Pat: The King has told me that the snakes have been terrorizing the leprechauns. It must stop.

Queen: Terrorizing the leprechauns is the only fun my snakes ever have. They don't mean any harm. There isn't anything to do around here!

St. Pat: Well, it simply must stop. There must be a better way to have fun. Let me think...I know, why not start a baseball team?

Queen: Don't be silly? How will the snakes hold the bat?

St. Pat: How about field hockey...or basketball or...

Queen: Silence! There just isn't anything to do here!

St. Pat: Well then leave, go someplace else like...San Franciso!

Queen: Where is San Francisco?

St. Pat: It's in America. There are all kinds of things to do. A lot of tourists. It's a great place I hear.

Queen: Sounds like a terrific idea. We'll do it!

St. Pat: Great, I'll tell the King.

SCENE 3

The next day all the snakes, including the Queen, board a boat headed for San Franciso. St. Pat, Mrs. St. Pat, and all the leprechauns are there to see them off.

Leprechaun King: Have a great trip and a great time.

Queen: We'll have a swell time!

All the snakes cheer.

As the boat sails away, everybody cheers (snakes and leprechauns)
And that is how St. Pat drove the snakes out of Ireland (sort of!)

Appendix B

This is a sample calendar of sessions for the entire year. I have divided each month into four weeks. Sometimes more than one session idea is given for a week. A plan for each session is included in this book, unless otherwise specified.

January

First week:	Names
Second Week:	Grab Bag Sing-A-Long
Third Week:	Spirituals (to honor Martin Luther King Jr's birthday)
Fourth Week:	Animals (since Ground Hog's Day is February 2nd)

February

First Week:	Music (National Music Month)
Second Week:	Love Songs (Valentine's Day)
Third Week:	Stephen Foster or Civil War (Lincoln's Birthday). The session plan is not included in the book.
Fourth Week:	Oriental Music (United Nation's Day)

March

First Week:	The Music of Bing Crosby
Second Week:	Irish Music/St. Patrick's Day
Third Week:	Springtime
Fourth Week:	Songs from the Movies/Academy Awards

April

First Week:	April Showers/Rain
Second Week:	Humor and Parody (National Laugh Week)
Third Week:	Country Western
Fourth Week:	Flower Songs/May Day (May 1st)

May

First Week:	*Cinco de Mayo (May 5th)*
Second Week:	*Mothers*
Third Week:	*The Music of Irving Berlin (birthday – May11th)*
Fourth Week:	*Sailors and Boats (National Maritime Day-May 22nd) This session is not included in the book.*

June

First Week:	*Rainbows and Clouds*
Second Week:	*The Music of Judy Garland (birthday-June 10th)*
Third Week:	*Fathers and Home*
Fourth Week:	*Summertime*

July

First Week:	*Patriotic Music (Fourth of July)*
Second Week:	*The Music of George Cohan*
Third Week:	*Hometown, U.S.A.*
Fourth Week:	*Travel*

August

First Week:	*Smiles (National Smile Week)*
Second Week:	*Hawaii*
Third Week:	*The Music of Johnny Mercer*
Fourth Week:	*A Session About Women (ratification of 19th amendment)*

September

First Week:	*Labor Day/Work Songs*
Second Week:	*School Days/Childhood Memories*
Third Week:	*The Music of Al Jolson (Jewish holidays)*
Fourth Week:	*The Music of George Gershwin (birthday September 26)*

Appendix B

October
    First Week: *Autumn/Moon Songs*
    Second Week: *Discoveries and Inventions (Discoverer's Day-October 12)*
    Third Week: *Time (Daylight Savings time changes)*
    Fourth Week: *Halloween Session*

November
    First Week: *Election Songs*
    Second Week: *Songs America Sang At War (Veteran's Day)*
    Third Week: *Body Parts*
    Fourth Week: *Colonial Music/Thanksgiving*

December
    First Week: *The Songs of Walt Disney (birthday-December 5th)*
    Second Week: *Winter*
    Third Week: *International Christmas (session not included)*
    Fourth Week: *Christmas Songs*

NOTE: Since Easter is a floating holiday, it is not included in this calendar. It can easily fit wherever the holiday falls in a given year.

Appendix C

Cross-Reference of Objectives

To provide an opportunity for reminiscing 2, 11, 14, 16, 19, 25, 26, 38, 44, 46, 50, 54, 55, 56, 62, 71, 75, 80, 82, 87, 102, 104, 105

To increase verbalization 2, 3, 6, 8, 9, 11, 14, 18, 20, 23, 25, 26, 29, 31, 36, 38, 41, 44, 55, 56, 60, 63, 67, 69, 82, 87, 95, 96, 101, 106, 107, 110

To increase attention span 2, 4, 15, 28, 33, 49, 52, 64, 71, 91, 100

To provide an atmosphere for creative self-expression 5, 6, 9, 18, 20, 21, 23, 26, 29, 30, 36, 46, 60, 62, 68, 74, 79, 100

To encourage self-disclosure 5, 29, 36, 38, 40, 43, 44, 60, 68, 69, 71, 74, 79, 80, 82, 88, 89, 90, 95, 96, 98, 100, 101, 104, 110, 113

To elevate mood 5, 12, 14, 29, 35, 39, 41, 63, 66, 73, 80, 81, 91, 100, 103

To provide an opportunity for choice 8, 24, 25, 31, 110

To encourage gross motor movement 4, 11, 14, 16, 18, 19, 23, 24, 27, 28, 30, 33, 34, 35, 42, 49, 51, 52, 54, 57, 60, 64, 67, 74, 75, 76, 78, 83, 84, 85, 86, 92, 95, 97, 100, 102, 104, 109, 111

To encourage fine motor movement 11, 14, 38, 71, 84, 111

To provide an opportunity for reality orientation 6, 11

To increase group interaction 47, 63, 110

To increase self-esteem...............................21, 29, 44, 47, 62

To increase contentment with the environment.......................23

To create an atmosphere where desires can be expressed 25

To explore common interests 3, 26

To provide an opportunity for teamwork 33

To provide a forum to express patriotic feelings

To improve affect 47

To reduce self-pity 12, 14, 29, 35, 41, 81, 91, 93, 100

To provide purposeful and directed sensory stimulation 11, 64, 72, 85

To improve impulse control 16, 33

To stimulate cognitive functioning 1, 2, 4, 9, 11, 14, 15, 16, 18, 19, 24, 25, 28, 31, 38, 40, 43, 49, 51, 53, 54, 55, 56, 64, 65, 68, 71, 74, 76, 79, 85, 87, 90, 92, 103, 106, 110

INDEX

Academy Awards/Movies 19
Andrews Sisters 51, 58, 109
Animals 3
April Showers (Rain) 27, 37, 53, 58, 84, 88, 94, 99, 100, 121
Autumn 1, 2, 123
Berlin, Irving 48, 56, 75, 109, 120
Body Parts 59, 123
Cinco de Mayo/Mexican-Latin American
. 63-65
Cohan, George M 15, 41
Cole, Nat "King" .57
Colonial Music/Thanksgiving 59-60, 115-116, 123
Country Western Music 26, 121
Crosby, Bing 16, 51, 54, 120
Disney, Walt 34-35, 121
Easter 10-11, 48, 56, 123
Fathers/Home 68-69, 122
Garland, Judy 53, 55-57, 122
Gershwin, George 49, 76, 122
Halloween .13-14, 122
Hawaii 8, 70-72, 122
Humor and Parody 73, 121
Irish Music/St. Patrick's Day 16-19, 37, 42, 47, 54-55, 59, 121
Ives, Burl/Folk Music 28, 75, 105
Jewish Music 76-77, 122
Jolson, Al 53, 77, 82, 95, 122

Kern, Jerome .45, 50
Love Songs 78, 95, 121
Mardi Gras 80
Mercer, Johnny 50, 122
Mills Brothers .58, 82
Mother 58, 82-83
Music 2, 21, 25
Names 21, 23, 119
Oriental Music 84-85, 114
Patriotic Music 39, 41, 114, 122
Rainbows and Clouds 43, 45, 46, 50, 56, 100, 122
School Days: Childhood Memories 122
Smiles 8, 47, 108, 122
Songs America Sang At War 122
The Sound of Music 90
Spirituals 92, 121
Springtime 94-95, 105, 121
Summer 24, 57, 102-103, 114
Time 96-98
Trains and Railroads 84-85
Travel 24-26, 122
Weather 88, 99
Winter 99, 101-102, 123
Women 105-107, 122
Working/Labor Day 110-111, 121
1960's 112-113

OTHER RESOURCES FROM ELDER BOOKS

ACTIVITY IDEAS FOR THE BUDGET MINDED

by Debra Cassistre

This popular treasury of tried and true activity ideas is now back by popular demand in a revised and expanded edition. Already used by thousands of activity directors, this new edition is packed with dozens of hands-on, ready to use, budget-stretching activities. These low cost activity ideas will give your program an inexpensive boost, create variety and give residents the kind of stimulation and entertainment they deserve. **$10.95**

FAILURE-FREE ACTIVITIES FOR THE ALZHEIMER'S PATIENT

by Carmel Sheridan

This award-winning book describes hundreds of simple, non-threatening activities which are suitable for persons with Alzheimer's disease. The author describes how to focus on the abilities that remain rather than the patient's deficits and shows how to create activities which capitalize on existing strengths. **$10.95**

FREE THINGS FOR ACTIVITY DIRECTORS

by Debra Cassistre

This revised and expanded edition of Debra Cassistre's book lists hundreds of items that can be obtained free—including books, games, posters, movies and craft items. It's message is clear and simple: activity directors can create a quality program with exciting resources even if they are on a tight budget. **$10.95**

REMINISCENCE: UNCOVERING A LIFETIME OF MEMORIES

by Carmel Sheridan

Reminiscing is one of the most powerful healing activities for people with Alzheimer's disease. This book explains the simple techniques involved in stimulating memories. It outlines themes to explore as well as hundreds of meaningful activities involving reminiscence. **$12.95**

TELL ME A STORY

Designed to encourage conversation through storytelling, reminiscence and some role play, *Tell Me A Story* can be used with individuals or groups. Very useful for family members who find it difficult to initiate conversation with an older adult, the kit contains 56 'conversation' cards set in large type. **$10.95**

ORDER FORM

Send To:
Elder Books   Post Office Box 490   Forest Knolls CA 94933
PH: 415 488-9002   FAX: 415 488-4720

Please send me:

Qty.		Price/copy	Totals
____	So Much More Than A Sing-A-Long	@ **$16.95**	$_____.___
____	Activity Ideas for the Budget Minded	@ **$10.95**	$_____.___
____	Failure-Free Activities	@ **$10.95**	$_____.___
____	Free Things for Activity Directors	@ **$10.95**	$_____.___
____	Reminiscence	@ **$12.95**	$_____.___
____	Tell Me A Story	@ **$10.95**	$_____.___
	Total for books		$_____.___
	Total sales tax		$_____.___
	Total shipping		$_____.___
	Amount enclosed		$_____.___

Shipping: $2.50 for first book, $1.25 for each additional book;
California residents, please add 8.25% sales tax.

Name

Address

City   State   Zip